كِتَاب

Political Tho

From the literature of

.

Hizb ut-Tahrir

Al- Khilafah Publications
PO Box 1100
London CR4 2ZR
Tel: 0956 245968
e-mail:info@khilafah.com
website:http://www.khilafah.com

Al- Khilafah Publications
PO Box 1100
London CR4 2ZR
Tel: 0956 245968
e-mail: info@khilafah.com
website: http://www.khilafah.com

1420 AH / 1999 CE

ISBN 1 899574 077

Translation of the Qur'an

It should be perfectly clear that the Qur'an is only authentic in it's original language, Arabic. Since perfect translation of the Qur'an is impossible, we have used the translation of the meaning of the Qur'an' throughout the book, as the result is only a crude meaning of the Arabic text.

Qur'anic *ayat* and transliterated
words have been *italicised*.

Ahadith appear in **bold**

ﷻ - subhanahu wa ta'ala
ﷺ - sallallahu 'alaihi wa sallam
ra - radhi allaho anha
AH - After Hijrah
CE - Common Era

Contents

Introduction

Politics means the taking care of the affairs of the *Ummah* internally and externally; it is performed by the State and the *Ummah*. The State handles this taking care (of the *Ummah*'s affairs) practically, and the *Ummah* accounts the State (re it's performance).

Ever since the Khilafah was destroyed and *Kufr* political systems were applied in the Islamic lands, Islam ceased to be political. In it's place came Western political thought established upon the Capitalist doctrine, a doctrine that detaches religion from life. What must be clearly understood by the Muslim *Ummah* is that taking care of the affairs by Islam cannot happen without the Khilafah and that separating political Islam from life and from the deen means eradicating Islam, it's systems and rules and the wiping out of the *Ummah*, her values, civilisation and message.

The capitalist states adopt the doctrine of detaching the deen from life and politics, and they work actively to spread this doctrine and establish it's rules upon the Muslim *Ummah*. They also work to mislead the *Ummah* and convince her that politics and the deen do not mix, and that politics means realism and being content with the current situation and the impossibility of changing it. All this is to ensure that the *Ummah* remains under the yoke of the states of *Kufr*, oppression and tyranny, and unable to envisage the path for revival. In addition they work to alienate Muslims from the Islamic political groups and from involvement in politics. This is because the *Kufr* states know that there is no way to strike against the West's political thoughts and rules except by political action and by being involved in politics on the basis of Islam. This campaign to alienate the Muslims from politics and politicians has reached the extent of depicting politics as contradictory to the greatness and spirituality of Islam. Therefore, the *Ummah* has to understand the secret behind the war fought by the infidel states and the puppet rulers against the Islamic groups, who are working to revive the Muslims by establishing the Khilafah State, fighting the *Kufr* thoughts and restoring the glory of Islam.

Therefore, it is a must that the Muslim *Ummah* understands clearly the meaning of politics linguistically and in Shari'ah, and that political Islam cannot exist without the Khilafah State. Without it, Islam ceases to be political. Nor can it be considered alive except when this State in it's capacity as an executive political entity implements and executes the Islamic rules. This is the Shari'ah method by which the Islamic rules and systems are executed in the public life. They have also to know that Allah 🕮 has obliged the *Ummah* to implement these rules, and forbade arbitration to *Kufr* systems due to their contradiction with Islam and as they are man-made.

Therefore, it is necessary to culture the *Ummah* with the Islamic culture and to continually inject her with the Islamic political thoughts and rules and explain how these thoughts and rules emanate from the Islamic Aqeedah in it's capacity as a political thought. It is also necessary to concentrate this culture from it's spiritual aspect in it's capacity as the commands and prohibitions of Allah 🕮 without reference to any other consideration. This spiritual aspect will guarantee the strength of the Islamic thoughts and rules within the souls, and manifest the meaning of politics and political thought to the *Ummah*, such that she perceives the responsibility placed on her shoulder to initiate the Islamic thoughts and rules in practical life, and the importance of the universal message that Allah 🕮 obliged her to carry to the world. This is particularly important as she sees the level she has reached in the present time, due to the disappearance of the Islamic state and the thoughts and rules of Islam from her life, and the level which the world has sunk to in terms of evil, misery and the enslaving of humanity. This political culturing, whether it is culturing by the Islamic thoughts and rules or by following the political events, will create the political awareness and cause the *Ummah* to shoulder her fundamental mission and original responsibility, which is to carry the Islamic Da'wa to all peoples and nations.

1
Political Thought

Political thought is of the highest types of thought. Political thought is that which is concerned with taking care of the affairs of the *Ummah*. The highest level of political thought is that which is related to man and the world from a particular point of view.

The Islamic Aqeedah is a political idea, so it is a political thought; indeed it is the foundation of the political thought for Muslims. It is an ideology, a system and a Deen, part of which is the state. The Islamic Aqeedah is distinguished from other Aqeedahs and ideologies in that it is spiritual and political. The thoughts and rules which emanate from it address the affairs of this world as well as the Hereafter. The point of view shaped by the Islamic Aqeedah differs from all points of view shaped by other ideologies and systems. Similarly, it's thoughts and rules differ from all other thoughts and rules existent in the world. Such differences exist in the foundation from which they stem, in their sources of legislation, and in their entireties as well as their details. The Islamic Aqeedah brought thoughts and rules addressing all of life's affairs, and the human relations in it. It looks after these affairs and relationships whether related to ruling, economics, social relations, education, internal or external policies of a state, or be they related to the relationship between the ruler and the ruled or the relationship of the state with other states, nations or peoples. Therefore, the political Aqeedah of Islam is complete and comprehensive; it addresses all affairs and aspects of life and treats all situations accurately.

Allah ﷻ says:

$$\text{وَنَزَّلْنَا عَلَيْكَ الْكِتَابَ تِبْيَانًا لِكُلِّ شَيْءٍ}$$

"And we have revealed to you The Book explaining all matters".[An-Nahl: 89]

He 🕋 also says:

$$\text{الْيَوْمَ أَكْمَلْتُ لَكُمْ دِينَكُمْ وَأَتْمَمْتُ}$$
$$\text{عَلَيْكُمْ نِعْمَتِي وَرَضِيتُ لَكُمُ الْإِسْلَامَ}$$

"Today I have completed your Deen for you, encompassed my blessings upon you, and have accepted Islam to you as a Deen". [Al- Maidah: 3]

The absence of the thoughts and rules that emanate from the Aqeedah has had the greatest impact on the life of Muslims. The Ottoman states adopting ideas and rules from non-Islamic sources and considering them as part of Islam even by name, and the negligence in adhering to the divine rules by individuals in their lives, were considered the most important factors in destroying the Islamic state and bringing the Muslims to such a level of humiliation and decline. Therefore, it is of extreme importance that Muslims completely adhere to the thoughts and divine rules, for they lead to the controlled behaviour of individuals as well as of the *Ummah* in the running of the state.

The rules which emanate from the political Islamic Aqeedah oblige the Muslims to implement Islam completely, and to establish upon it's basis an independent and distinguished Islamic entity and to build a unique society which is the Islamic society. They also oblige Muslims to be one Islamic *Ummah* regardless of their ethnic background and colour, united by the Islamic Aqeedah which unifies their viewpoint about life, namely the Halal and Haram, which makes this viewpoint a yardstick for their view towards incidents and events, and for judging them under one single state.

Furthermore, the Islamic Aqeedah obliges Muslims as parties, groups and organisations to work to resume the Islamic way of life and carry the Islamic Da'wah i.e. to resolve the vital issue of the Muslims. The resumption of the Islamic way of life means the return of Muslims to the Islamic way of life in *Dar-ul-Islam*, an Islamic society dominated by the Islamic thoughts and emotions and ruled by the systems and rules of Islam. In this society, all of life's affairs are run in accordance with the divine rules under the Islamic Khilafah state. In the Khilafah state, Muslims appoint a Khaleefah who is given the *Bayah* for obedience as long as he rules by the Book of Allah, the Sunnah of His Messenger and carries the Islamic message to mankind through Da'wah and Jihad.

For the Muslim *Ummah* today to achieve revival, she must make the Islamic Aqeedah the basis for her life and establish ruling and authority on that basis. In other words, she must address the daily problems by the rules that emanate from this Aqeedah i.e. by the divine rules solely in their capacity as commands and prohibitions from Allah. Only then will revival be achieved with certainty. As a matter of fact, not only will revival take place but the true revival will occur. Only then will the *Ummah* return to her previous position of glory and world leadership. Therefore, the *Ummah* must be cultured by the political culture starting before anything else with it's rational Aqeedah i.e. it's comprehensive idea about the universe, man and life. This Aqeedah must be taught as a political idea and not only as a spiritual idea. Then all political thoughts that emanate from it, as well as the means and goals which are built on it must be part of that culture (to the *Ummah*).

The Islamic *Ummah* embraces the Islamic Aqeedah as a comprehensive idea about the universe, man and life, as a political Aqeedah, as an intellectual leadership and basis, and as a specific viewpoint on life. Therefore, upon witnessing the entire world, including herself, in disarray, suffering under political and economic injustice, enslaved by tyrant powers, and living a nightmare of hardship, enslavement and humiliation, the *Ummah* is obliged to take upon her shoulders the responsibility of saving the world and bringing it out of the darkness of mis-guidance and deception to the light of guidance and happiness. Though the *Ummah* suffers under the tyrant power she is not permitted to think of herself only. Selfishness does not relate to her beliefs and is alien to her deep-rooted values and thoughts. Therefore, she must think of saving the world as well as herself and she must change herself and liberate the world, and not work for herself alone. This is because she is part of this world, and she exists in order to guide mankind. Once she embraced the Aqeedah of Islam, it became an obligation upon her to save mankind from misery, injustice, humiliation and enslavement.

The Muslim *Ummah* embraces a political idea about life, and she embraces a method to implement this idea in life. Once a nation possesses the correct idea and it's method, then without a doubt, it becomes worthy of disseminating goodness and worthy of carrying the leadership of this idea. Due to this, not only is the *Ummah* capable of achieving true revival, but she is also able to be the source of goodness for others and carry this idea to the people both as an intellectual leadership and a certain viewpoint about life. Consequently, through the carrying of the Islamic Da'wah to all peoples and nations she is capable of solving the problem of the world and saving it from the misery, enslavement and humiliation that it is drowning in.

2
Politics

olitics or *Siyasah* is looking after the affairs of the *Ummah* (nation) internally and externally. It is carried out by the state and the *Ummah*. The state is the entity that engages in this caring in practice while the *Ummah* engages in it by taking the state to task.

This definition of politics exists among all people, for it describes the reality of politics as a term. It is like the definition of the mind, truthfulness and authority, among others. Each meaning has a common reality for all people and therefore has a common meaning for them, for it is a comprehended reality. However, they differ in the rules that govern such a reality. Moreover, the linguistic meaning of this word in the root verb *Sasa, Yasoosu, Siyasatan* is to care for ones affairs. The author of Al-Qamoos Al-Muheet, (an Arabic dictionary) says, and *sustu ar-raiyata siyasatan* means commanded her and forbade her. This definition can also be extracted from the Ahadith addressing the rulers responsibility, the obligation of taking him to task and the importance of caring for the interests of Muslims. The Messenger ﷺ said: "**Any person Allah has placed in (a position) to foster the peoples affairs and he does not give them his advice he will not even smell the scent of *Jannah* (paradise).** And the saying of the Messenger ﷺ: **Anyone who took charge of any Muslims and he died while he was deceiving them Allah will prevent him from entering paradise (*Jannah*).** And: **There will be leaders over you, (who will do things) you recognise (as part of the Deen), and you don't recognise. Whoever recognised he would be relieved (of sin), and whoever denied (the wrong), he would be safe. But what about he who accepted and followed.** They said: Shouldn't we fight against them. He ﷺ said: **No, as long as they prayed. And Whoever awakens and his concern is not for Allah, he does not belong to Allah.** And: **Whoever awakens not concerned with Muslims (affairs) is not from them.** Jareer ibn Abdullah said: I gave a pledge to the Prophet 🌸 to establish the prayer, to give the alms, and to give advice to every Muslim. Jareer Ibn Abdullah also said: I came to the Prophet 🌸 and said: I give a pledge to you on Islam. The Messenger placed the condition upon me to give advice to every Muslim. These Ahadith, whether pertaining to the ruler in his position of ruling, or to the *Ummah*'s questioning of the ruler, or those dealing with the relationship between the Muslims with each other as far as caring for their interests and giving them the sincere advice is concerned, they all give the definition of politics as: fostering the *Ummah*'s affairs. Therefore, the definition of politics is a divine definition derived from the Shari'ah evidences.

With regard to the caring for the affairs of the *Ummah* in practice, Shar'a has given the ruler alone that responsibility. Neither the citizens, collectively or anyone of them individually is allowed to carry out such tasks, unless he is legitimately appointed to do so. Such legitimate appointment can be made through a pledge of allegiance from the people as is the case with the Khaleefah. Appointment can also be made by the Khaleefah himself or by any of those who are authorised by the Khaleefah to make appointments like his assistants and the Governors (Walis). Anyone who is not appointed by the pledge of allegiance (from the citizens) or by the Khaleefah is not allowed to carry out any of the affairs of the *Ummah*, either internally or externally.

Authority and caring for the peoples affairs is designated by the Shari'ah exclusively to the ruler. Allah's Messenger 🌸 said: **"Whoever sees something he dislikes from his Ameer, he should be patient with him, for anyone who rebels against the authority and dies in that state (of rebellion), he will die in a state of *Jahiliyah*** (ignorance)." This Hadith makes rebellion against him a rebellion against the authority. This means authority belongs to the Ameer, and no one else. Allah's Messenger 🌸 also said: **"The children of Israel were looked after by their prophets. Whenever a prophet died, another succeeded him, but there will be no prophet after me. There will be Khulafaa and they will number many."** This means that your affairs, Oh Muslims, will be cared for by the Khulafaa. Thus, the ones who care for the Muslims affairs have been specified. These Ahadith indicate that none other than the Ameer has the authority and no one is allowed to care for the peoples affairs except the Khulafaa. This proves that caring for the citizen's affairs is for the ruler exclusively. Furthermore, the Messenger's action shows that caring for the peoples affairs and the authority are restricted to him as a head of state. It was he ﷺ who used to delegate authority and caretaking actions to people. For example, the Messenger ﷺ appointed people to carry out his duties in Medina upon his departure for a *Ghazwa* (battle). He also appointed governors, judges, people to collect resources, people to perform certain public work such as the distribution of water, and the estimating of fruit's and produce, etc. The above is an evidence to restrict authority and caretaking to the ruler, i.e. the Khaleefah and whoever is assigned by the Khaleefah, and to the Ameer and whoever is appointed by the Ameer. The Sultan or authority is caring for the peoples affairs in a binding fashion. In other words, carrying out the rulers responsibilities is restricted to the ruler. Absolutely no one else is permitted to carry out these responsibilities. This is because the Shar'a delegated the authority and the task of caretaking to the sultan (Khaleefah) and whoever is appointed by the Khaleefah. If an individual other than the Imam or one appointed by the Imam, assumes the responsibility of ruling and looking after the affairs of the people he will be acting against the Shar'a and thus his action would be *Batil* (invalid) and every invalid action is Haram. Therefore, it is not allowed for anyone other than the Khaleefah and whoever is appointed by the Khaleefah i.e. by other than the ruler, to perform any action of government and ruling. Such a person is not allowed to assume caretaking for the *Ummah* in a binding fashion, for this is the job of the ruler and no one else is allowed to perform it.

With regard to the internal policy of the Islamic state, it is based on implementing the rules of Islam internally. During the existence of the Islamic state, it carried out the rules of Islam in it's domain. It used to organise mutual relations, execute the punishment system (*Hudud*), protect ethics (*Akhlaq*), ensure the performance of the *Ibadat* (worships), and foster the affairs of all it's subjects in accordance to the Islamic laws.

Islam clarified the method of executing it's rules on those under it's authority, be they Muslims or non-Muslims. The Islamic state used to implement the rules of Islam in accordance with this method since the method of implementation is a divine rule (*Hukm Shari'ah*) in the same way that it is a solution to a problem. All people are addressed with Islam, for Allah ﷺ addressed all of mankind with it.

Allah ﷻ said:

$$\text{يَاأَيُّهَا الإِنسَانُ مَا غَرَّكَ بِرَبِّكَ الْكَرِيمِ}$$

"O man! What has seduced you from your Lord Most Beneficent". [Al- Infitar : 6]

Scholars of Usool-ul-fiqh stated that every sane person who understands the speech is addressed with the divine rules, whether he or she is a Muslim or non-Muslim. Imam al-Ghazali stated in his book Al-Mustasfa Fi Al-Usool: The addressed person is the one who is charged (*Mukallaf*). He/she must be a person who understands the speech. What qualifies someone as being subject to the rules is whether as a human being, the person's mind has the ability to understand the speech. Therefore, all mankind is addressed with Islam, an address of *Da'wah* as well as *Takleef* (legislation). The speech of *Da'wah* means calling all people to embrace Islam. The address of *Takleef* means obliging all people to act upon the rules of Islam.

Islam considers the group that is governed with this system as a human unit, regardless of it's race and ethnicity. To qualify for such a view, it only mandates citizenship (loyalty to the state and system). In Islam, there are no minorities. All people, as humans irrespective of any other consideration, are subjects of the Islamic state, as long as they are citizens of it. Therefore, the internal policy of the Islamic state is to implement the Islamic Shari'ah on all those who carry it's citizenship, be they Muslims or non-Muslims.

The foreign policy of the Islamic state is it's relationship with other states, peoples and nations. This relationship is the looking after of the *Ummah*'s affairs externally. This foreign policy is based on a fixed and non-changeable idea, namely to spread Islam to the world, to every nation and every people. This basis does not vary or change irrespective of any change in the individuals who are in power. This basis of foreign policy existed throughout history, from the time the Messenger ﷺ settled in Medina until the Ottoman state collapsed as the last Islamic state. Throughout history, this basis did not change at all. Since the Messenger ﷺ erected his state in Medina, he established it's relationship with other states on the basis of spreading Islam. So, he struck treaties with the Jews in order to enable himself to spread the Da'wah in Hijaz. Then he struck the treaty of Hudaibiyah with Quraysh to be able to spread the Da'wah in the Arabian Peninsula, establishing relations with them based on spreading Islam by inviting them to embrace it. In addition the Khulafaa that came after him established their relations with all the states on the basis of spreading Islam, and continued to carry the Da'wah of Islam to the world. The existence of the state is for no other reason but to implement Islam internally and carry it's Da'wah to the world externally. Consequently, the task of the Islamic state externally is solely and exclusively to carry the Islamic Da'wah. What makes the spreading of Islam the basis for the foreign policy is the fact that the Message of Muhammad is for all mankind. Allah says:

$$ وَمَا أَرْسَلْنَاكَ إِلاَّ كَافَّةً لِلنَّاسِ بَشِيرًا وَنَذِيرًا $$

"We have not sent you (O Muhammad) except as a giver of glad tidings and a warner to all mankind". [Saba: 28]

And Allah says:

$$ يَاأَيُّهَا النَّاسُ قَدْ جَاءَتْكُمْ مَوْعِظَةٌ مِنْ رَبِّكُمْ $$

"Oh mankind, and admonition from your Lord has come to you". [Yunus: 57]

He said:

$$ يَاأَيُّهَا النَّاسُ إِنِّي رَسُولُ اللَّهِ إِلَيْكُمْ جَمِيعًا $$

"Say Oh mankind, I am the Messenger of Allah to you all". [Al-Araf:158]

He also said:

$$ وَأُوحِيَ إِلَيَّ هَذَا الْقُرْآنُ لِأُنذِرَكُمْ بِهِ وَمَنْ بَلَغَ $$

"This Qur'an has been revealed to me by inspiration that I may warn you and all whom it reaches". [Al-Anam: 19]

The Messenger ﷺ conveyed the message to the people. After his death, his message, continued to be conveyed by the Muslims. Therefore, carrying the Islamic Da'wah to the world is a continuation of the work of the Messengers. That is why carrying the Islamic Da'wah is the basis of the Islamic state's relationship with other states, nations and peoples. This is defined by the Hukm Shari'ah, which is established by the Qur'an, Sunnah and Ijmaa us Sahabah. Consequently, the foreign policy of the Islamic state is to carry the Islamic Da'wah to the world.

The Islamic state implements this foreign policy via an established and non-changeable method, namely Jihad. This method does not change regardless of any changes to the people in authority. This method existed throughout history since the Messenger ﷺ settled in Medina until the last Islamic state was destroyed. The method never changed nor varied. Since the Messenger ﷺ established the state in Medina, he ﷺ prepared the army and initiated Jihad in order to remove the physical obstacles from it's way. The Quraysh were a physical barrier preventing the spread of the Islamic Da'wah, so they were determined to eliminate it. He ﷺ succeeded in eliminating the Quraysh as an entity in addition to other entities that prevented the spread of the Da'wah until Islam dominated the Arabian Peninsula. Then, the Islamic State started approaching other nations in order to spread Islam amongst them. However, it found that the acting ruling bodies stood as physical obstacles preventing the penetration of the Da'wah. Thus, it became necessary to remove these entities obstructing the path of the Da'wah so as to reach the people themselves and call them to Islam by ruling them by it. Ruling them by Islam will lead the people to see and experience the justice of Islam and comfort and tranquillity of living under it's flag. The people will be invited to embrace it in the best manner and without any compulsion or force. Jihad continued as the method to spread Islam. So, countries were conquered and kingdoms and states were removed by Jihad with Islam ruling the peoples and nations. Islam was embraced by hundreds of millions of people after it ruled them. Therefore, the method that was followed in the foreign policy was Jihad, which was fixed and non-changeable, and it will never change.

It is the duty of the Islamic state to engage itself in certain political actions. Some of these actions pertain to giving clear information about

Islam, disseminating the ideas of Islam and performing the Da'wah and propagation for Islam. Other political actions pertain to demonstrating the power and the ability of the Islamic state as well as the toughness and courage of Muslims. The Messenger 嶽 did many actions of this nature, where he 嶽 sent many people to the very heart of the lands of shirk to call them to Islam, such as the occasion when 40 men were sent to Najd to convey Islam. He 嶽 also used to show the might of the state as when he 嶽 paraded the Muslim army in Medina prior to departing to the Ghazwah of Tabuk. The Messenger 嶽 said: **"I was supported by terror from a month's distance march."** It is due to this that the Muslim army throughout history was feared. Therefore, the political action pertaining to the spread of the Islamic thoughts and showing the power of the state must be performed before fighting can take place.

While Jihad is the fixed and non-changeable method to spread Islam, political actions and designed (planned) manoeuvres are a must before engaging in fighting. This is a fundamental issue in establishing the relationship between the state and other states, peoples and nations in a specific fashion. Also, good neighbourly relations or economic relations makes the spread of Islam easier. Consequently, the political idea that the Islamic state's relationship with other states, nations and peoples is based upon is to spread Islam among them and carry Islam to them. The method to achieve this is Jihad in the way of Allah (*Fi sabeel Allah*).

With regard to questioning the state by the *Ummah*, Islam made it mandatory on Muslims to take the rulers to task. The fact that Islam obliged Muslims to obey them even if they are unjust or take peoples rights, does not mean remaining silent regarding their behaviour. Rather, they should be obeyed and should be questioned for their actions and behaviour. Allah 嶽 obliged the Muslims to question the rulers. He 嶽 also decisively ordered them to force change on the rulers if they took the peoples rights or did not fulfil their duties toward them, or neglected any of their affairs, went against any rule of Islam or ruled by other than that which Allah 嶽 revealed. Muslim reported that Ummu Salamah said that Allah's Messenger 嶽 said: **"There will be leaders over you, (who will do things) you recognise (as part of the Deen), and you don't recognise. Whoever recognised that would be relieved (of sin), and whoever denied (the wrong), he would be safe but what about the one who accepted and followed"**. They said: Shouldn't we fight against

them. He ﷺ said: **"No, as long as they prayed."** In another narration
**"Whoever recognised he would be relieved (of sin), and whoever
denied (the wrong) he would be safe, but what about the one who
accepted and followed"**. This narration explains the other one. The
Messenger ﷺ ordered to deny the ruler in any method that is within ones
ability: with the hand as long as it does not escalate to physical fighting,
with the mouth using any permissible statement, or with the heart if
unable to do the first two. The Messenger ﷺ considered that whoever
does not deny the *Haram* actions of the ruler is a partner in the sin, for
he ﷺ said: **"Whoever accepted what they did and submitted to that,
then he would not be safe from the sin"**.

Furthermore, the evidences of commanding good and forbidding evil
are evidences for the obligation of questioning the ruler, for they are
general and thus include the ruler as well as others. Allah ﷻ commanded
us to command goodness and forbid evil in a decisive manner.
He ﷻ said:

$$\text{وَلْتَكُنْ مِنْكُمْ أُمَّةٌ يَدْعُونَ إِلَى الْخَيْرِ وَيَأْمُرُونَ بِالْمَعْرُوفِ وَيَنْهَوْنَ عَنِ الْمُنْكَرِ وَأُولَئِكَ هُمُ الْمُفْلِحُونَ}$$

*"And let there arise amongst you a group, inviting to all that is good (Islam),
commanding al-Marouf (good) and forbidding al-Munkar (evil); and those are the
ones whom are the successful"* [Al- Imran: 104]

$$\text{الَّذِينَ إِنْ مَكَّنَّاهُمْ فِي الأَرْضِ أَقَامُوا الصَّلاةَ وَآتَوُا الزَّكَاةَ وَأَمَرُوا بِالْمَعْرُوفِ وَنَهَوْا عَنِ الْمُنْكَرِ}$$

*"Those who, if We firmly establish them on earth, remain constant in prayer, and give
in charity, and command what is right and forbid the doing of what is wrong"*.
[Al- Hajj: 41]

وَالْمُؤْمِنُونَ وَالْمُؤْمِنَاتُ بَعْضُهُمْ
أَوْلِيَاءُ بَعْضٍ يَأْمُرُونَ
بِالْمَعْرُوفِ وَيَنْهَوْنَ عَنِ الْمُنْكَرِ

*"And the believers, both men and women, they are protecting friends one to another;
they command what is right and forbid what is wrong".* [At- Tauba: 71]

كُنتُمْ خَيْرَ أُمَّةٍ أُخْرِجَتْ لِلنَّاسِ
تَأْمُرُونَ بِالْمَعْرُوفِ وَتَنْهَوْنَ
عَنِ الْمُنْكَرِ

*"You are the best Ummah raised to mankind, you command what is right and
forbid what is wrong".* [Al- Imran: 110]

الَّذِينَ يَتَّبِعُونَ الرَّسُولَ النَّبِيَّ
الأُمِّيَّ الَّذِي يَجِدُونَهُ مَكْتُوبًا
عِنْدَهُمْ فِي التَّوْرَاةِ وَالإنجيل
يَأْمُرُهُمْ بِالْمَعْرُوفِ وَيَنْهَاهُمْ
عَنِ الْمُنْكَرِ

*"Those who follow the (last) Messenger, the unlettered Prophet whom they find
mentioned in the Torah and Gospel; He commands them of what is right and forbids
them what is wrong"* [Al- Araf: 157]

التَّائِبُونَ الْعَابِدُونَ الْحَامِدُونَ
السَّائِحُونَ الرَّاكِعُونَ السَّاجِدُونَ
الآمِرُونَ بِالْمَعْرُوفِ وَالنَّاهُونَ
عَنِ الْمُنْكَرِ

*"(It is a triumph of) those who turn (unto Allah) in repentance and who worship and
praise (Him), and wander in devotion to the cause of Allah, and bow down (before
Him) and prostrate themselves in adoration, and command what is right and forbid
what is wrong".* [At- Tauba: 112]

Allah ﷻ ordered us in the above ayaat to command goodness and forbid evil. This order was attached with the connotation (*Qareenah*) that makes such orders decisive, namely the praise for doing it. He ﷻ said: And those are the successful ones, you are the best *Ummah* and the repenters, the worshippers, among others. The presence of these connotations (*Qareenahs*) makes the order decisive which means an obligation. Also, questioning the ruler is only commanding him to do good and forbidding him from doing evil and therefore, it is an obligation. There are also numerous Ahadith directing us to command good and forbid evil. Huthayfah b. al-Yaman said that the Prophet ﷺ said: **"By the One in whose hand is my soul, you have to command the good and forbid the evil or Allah will be about to send a punishment upon you then you will ask Him for help and He will not answer you."** Abu Said Al-Khudri said: Allah's Messenger ﷺ said: **"Whoever of you sees evil, let him change it with his hand, and if not able then with his mouth and if he is still not able then let him hate it within his heart and that is the least of faith."** Also Uday b. Umayrah said: I heard the Prophet ﷺ say: **"Allah does not punish the general public because of the wrong doing of specific people until they see the evil (committed) among them while able to stop it and they do not. If they do that, Allah will punish the specific people and the general public."**

The above Ahadith make commanding good and forbidding evil an obligation. These Ahadith oblige the Muslims to command the rulers to do good and forbid them from doing evil. Undoubtedly, this is the very action of questioning them for their actions.

However, there are Ahadith that address questioning the ruler specifically due to the importance of commanding him to do good and forbidding him from evil. Atiyyah reported that Abu Said said: Allah's Messenger ﷺ said: **"The best jihad is a word of truth to an unjust ruler."** Abu Umamah reported that: A man approached Allah's Messenger ﷺ at the first Jamrah (in Hajj) and asked him: Oh Messenger of Allah, which is the best jihad? The Messenger ﷺ remained silent. When the Messenger threw the second stone, the man asked him again. The Messenger did not reply. Upon throwing the stone of Aqbah, and the Messenger was about to mount, he ﷺ said: **"Where is the questioner"?** He said: Here I am Oh Messenger of Allah. He ﷺ said: **"A**

word of truth said to an unjust ruler." This is an explicit text pertaining to the ruler and the obligation of saying the truth to him, i.e. questioning him. Struggling against those rulers who take peoples rights or fall short in their duties or neglect any of the *Ummah*'s affairs or do the like of that is an obligation. This is because Allah ﷻ demanded it and considered it like jihad. Rather, He ﷻ made it the best type of jihad; since Muhammad ﷺ said the best jihad is struggling against the tyrant ruler. This in itself is sufficient to prove that it is an obligation to question the rulers.

The Messenger ﷺ encouraged the struggle against the unjust rulers regardless of the harm that is inflicted upon the person who does so. The Muslim is encouraged to do it even if it leads to his death. It was reported that the Messenger ﷺ said: "**The master of martyrs is Hamzah and a man who stood up to an unjust ruler, commanding him (to do good) and forbidding him (from evil) and was killed**". This is one of the most emphatic forms commanding the Muslims to endure harm, even death, in the process of questioning the ruler and struggling against the unjust rulers.

3
Political Concepts

U nderstanding the foreign policy is an essential requirement to protect the entity of the state and the *Ummah*. It is also a fundamental prerequisite to be able to carry the Da'wah to the world, and a necessary action to organise the *Ummah*'s relationship with others in the correct fashion.

Since the Islamic *Ummah* is obliged to carry the Islamic Da'wah to all mankind, it is mandatory upon Muslims to set their relations with the world, beware of it's conditions, comprehend it's problems, be knowledgeable of the motives of states and peoples, follow up the political actions in the world, observe the political plans of the states in terms of the styles used to execute their plans, and the manner of their relationships with each other, as well as the political manoeuvres carried out by these states. Therefore, it is a must that Muslims realise the reality of the situation in the Muslim world in the light of the understanding of the international situation in order to know the actions and styles needed to establish their state and carry out their Da'wah to the world.

Consequently, it becomes essential that Muslims completely understand the international situation and the details related to it. They also must comprehend the position of the existing states in the world that have weight in the general international situation.

All states are enemies to Islam, since they embrace religions and ideologies opposed to Islam, and carry a point of view that not only differs but is diametrically opposed to the Islamic point of view. The superpowers specifically are more than enemies, for they have interests in the Islamic lands. It is due to these interests, that they destroyed the Islamic state in order to finish the Islamic *Ummah*. They set up long term plans aimed at preventing the return of the Islamic *Ummah* to her glorious place amongst other nations. Naturally, the superpowers are busy designing plans and spending efforts to bury the Islamic state in it's cradle before the Islamic *Ummah* moves. They will continue to struggle against the Islamic *Ummah*, it's presence and strength as long as the Islamic state is present or as long as those enemy states are strong, as states, as peoples or even as individuals.

If knowledge of every state's policy in the world is a matter that no Muslim politician can do without, knowledge of the nature, secrets, plans, styles and means of the superpowers, in general terms, is of extreme importance to every Muslim. Detailed and practical knowledge of these matters, following up the various changing daily events, with the complete realisation of the bases and foundations of the policies of the superpowers is an essential for every Muslim politician and thinker. This serves the purpose of understanding the dangers to shield the *Ummah* from them, thus securing the state and the Islamic *Ummah* and the carrying of the Islamic Da'wah to the world.

4
Politics is the Art of Possibilities

Politics is about ideas related to fostering peoples affairs. These ideas may be bases, creeds, rules, actions that are taking place, took place, or will take place or news. If these ideas are addressing a matter of reality, then it is politics, be it contemporary or futuristic. If it occurred in the past, i.e. it was a reality in the past, whether recent or ancient, it is history. That is why history was politics and later became history. This history could have been facts that do not change with the circumstances and therefore must be studied. Or it could have been incidents that occurred in certain circumstances and therefore must not be taken into consideration. The reader must be aware of this latter type of history when reading it so as not to adopt that event in other than the circumstances in which it occurred, for he will fall in error and harm will occur if taken.

A human being or an individual living this life is a politician who likes politics and coexists with it. This is because he takes care of his own affairs or the affairs of those whom he is responsible for, or his *Ummah*'s, the ideology's affairs or his own ideas. However, individuals, groups, states or international alliances who champion fostering the affairs of their nations, states, region or countries are politicians by their human nature. They are politicians due to the nature of their work, life and policies. And because of this, they become outstanding politicians, and are the ones rightfully called politicians. This term is not given to an ordinary person since he is limited in his thinking in terms of looking after the affairs, as well as limited in action in life. Discussion in politics concerns politicians, not all individuals.

Scholars defined politics as the art of the possible. This is a correct definition, however, it is erroneous to restrict it to immediate issues because it means realism in the wrong sense of the word which is studying the situation and addressing it as it is. If this idea was correct, there would be no history or political life. This is because history charts the changing of a situation and political life is changing the ongoing events. Therefore, defining politics as the art of the possible is wrong if understood as the people and politicians understand it. However, as far as the word possible is concerned, if it is understood in it's true meaning which is that which is opposed to the impossible then it is true, for politics is not the art of the impossible, rather the art of the possible only. Ideas that are not related to possible events and reality are not political, they are logical propositions or mere imagination. For ideas to be political, they must be related to the possible. That is why politics is the art of the possible, not the impossible. Politics doesn't deal with the impossible and neither is it realism or practicality for that is against history. Had not the events changed according to what is possible then there would not have been politics, and history would not have existed for history is the changed situation. So politics is really the art of the possible as opposed to the impossible. The Messenger 鑾 viewed politics as the art of possibilities, meaning not the impossibilities, and because of this, he replaced shirk with Islam. The Islamic ideas and rules treated peoples problems and replaced the ideas of shirk and *Kufr*.

Imperialism, especially Western imperialism is very aware of Islam and it's threat if it returns to life. Thus, it put forward a realistic understanding for politics. Politics with this understanding of realism was circulated amongst Muslims and used as a basis for action by politicians. For them, politics is the art of the possible, i.e. acting according to the situation. Consequently, they started calling anything that was not part of the current situation as imagination and mere pipe dreams, in order to keep the Muslims away from Islam and it's thoughts. This also means giving in to the current situation and not thinking of changing it. Consequently, this current understanding (of politics) among the *Ummah* must be fought. It must also be comprehended that politics is fostering the *Ummah*'s affairs according to the rules of Islam, not according to the current situation or what is required by the current situation.

5
Politics and International Politics

Local politics, i.e. fostering the affairs of the *Ummah* and the state is important. However, it should not be the main focus of concern nor the only concern. Making local politics the main focus of concern leads to selfishness and working for one's self. It is also harmful because it leads to internal conflicts and struggle amongst politicians as well as groups and individuals, which can be damaging to the state and the *Ummah*. Furthermore, making local politics the only concern not only prevents people from comprehending the meaning of politics but also makes them negligent of the *Ummah*'s affairs and the politician has to look after the affairs of his *Ummah* to be a politician. This cannot be achieved except by being concerned with the affairs of other nations and states, and by being knowledgeable of their news and activities as well as gathering as much as possible of information about them.

Therefore, international and foreign politics is as inseparable a part of politics as politics itself. It is only politics when it is composed of ideas about fostering the affairs of one's own *Ummah* as well as the affairs of other nations and states. Consequently, the relationship between international and foreign politics with politics is that of a part to a whole, and can even be considered the essential component of it.

The foreign and international politics that one must be concerned with is that of the influential nations and states, particularly those that are related to one's *Ummah*, state or the creed that his state is based on and not all nations and states. Consequently, international and foreign politics merely mean the policy of the influential nations and states, particularly those that effect ones state and *Ummah*, whether this effect is direct or indirect.

Therefore, the entire Muslim *Ummah* and particularly the politicians must be occupied with guarding against external threats, i.e. she should be occupied with foreign and international politics by enhancing awareness and following up the affairs of other nations and observing all possibility of danger.

Moreover, the Islamic state doesn't consist solely of it's rulers, rather it is the *Ummah* that actually lives under the authority of the Khilafah state. So, the entire *Ummah* is the state. The *Kufr* states realise this fact and use it as a basis for their work. As long as the *Ummah* realises that it itself is the state, it will keep up with the news and affairs of other states and peoples in order to remain aware of it's enemies and to be prepared for them. Thus, news pertaining to foreign politics must always be well known and generally understood by the *Ummah* at large. It should also be the concern of politicians and intellectuals to inform the people of the foreign politics. The people in addition should choose their representatives in the *Ummah*'s Council for questioning and consultation on the basis of politics and international politics. Because this is what should be common among the *Ummah* and it's representatives in the Majlis of the *Ummah*. As for the politicians and intellectuals, generally speaking, knowing the foreign and international politics is the subject that should dominate their actions and ideas. This is because the Muslim is only created for Islam and the carrying of it's Da'wah. He/she only lives for this Deen, protecting it and spreading it. If Jihad is the pinnacle of Islam, then carrying the Islamic Da'wah is the goal that Jihad is initiated for. This peak requires knowledge of foreign and international politics.

Furthermore, any state that seeks to have an impact on the world and have influence and glory, must make the foreign policy one of it's fundamental issues, and it must use it's foreign policy as a means to enhance and strengthen it's position internally and externally. Due to this reality, politicians and intellectuals must comprehend foreign and international politics, whether they are rulers or not. This is what makes them politicians, i.e. people who take care of the affairs of the *Ummah*, because the important affairs of the *Ummah* depend on the foreign and international politics. Consequently, it is the duty of all political parties, politicians, intellectuals and scholars to make foreign and international politics the highest priority in their work.

It is not sufficient for politicians, intellectuals and scholars to know foreign and international politics in general, feeling satisfied with knowing the conclusions of events. While general knowledge is useful, it is not sufficient to anticipate coming threats and to protect the *Ummah*, nor to understand events, useful incidents, intentions and goals. Detailed knowledge and analysis of such actions, events, intentions and goals is therefore a necessity. In order to understand the enemy's intentions toward the state and *Ummah*, one must first be aware of the statement of the enemy and the circumstances in which the statement was made. Secondly, one must be aware of the enemies actions and the circumstances surrounding their actions. Thirdly, one must be aware of the enemy's relationships and the status of these relationships. Without the above three points, one cannot know the intentions of the enemy. Knowing the above three points requires details: statements made must be known in detail, kept up with, and followed up, so that their context is known. The same applies to actions and relationships. While the common people do not concern themselves with the details, the prominent members of the *Ummah*, particularly the politicians must be aware of them, for they are in charge of the *Ummah* and claim that they foster her affairs.

It is true that presently, international politics and the policies of the influential states are based on diplomacy, meaning contacts and agents. However, this is only temporary. Such a situation only exists due to the absence of a terrifying superpower in the world. When a terrifying superpower is present in the world, the situation will change and the international and influential states politics will depend heavily on political and military actions. Nonetheless, it's details should still be a subject of concern. Thus, if there exist agents, they should be known, even if they were from *Kufr* states and if contacts are made and political actions took place, they should be known in detail, especially covert actions.

Foreign and international politics, whether based on agents, contacts, political or military actions, must be well known in detail. This means knowing politics itself as well as intentions and goals and to understand the real meaning behind statements made, actions or relationships. If details are not known, politics will not be understood nor will the person be a politician and obviously, intentions and goals will not be known.

6
Understanding the International Situation

The international situation is constructed according to the existing relationships among the effective states on the international scene. Whilst states active on the international scene may number many, effective states are few. The effectiveness of the state is proportionate with that state's strength. Since a state's situation varies effectively due to it's strength and weakness, relations consequently also vary amongst these states. A change could occur due to war which weakens a participating state and it's influence on other states (on the international situation) thereby leading to another state rushing to replace it. Also, a change may take place during peace time through the gradual development of power. So a state may become weak and another may become stronger. However, war is more effective in making change. Due to the variation in a state's situation and strength, the international situation also changes. A change might take place in the participants or in the structure of relations. Since change in the situation and strength of influential states at the international stage is not rapid, it takes long periods of time for the international situation to change.

The strength of a state is not only dependent upon it's military might, it also relies on all it's material, intellectual and moral abilities and capabilities that it can muster from outside it's borders. So, a state's strength includes it's ideology or universal message which it carries to the world in addition to the military and economic strength it possesses as well as it's skill and shrewdness in executing political actions and diplomacy.

In a struggle between one state and others on the international stage, the state picks the strongest and most effective of it's tools at it's disposal, or at least, what it perceives to be the most effective, depending on the international situation. Ideological, military or economic strength all have the potential to achieve and maintain the interests as well as establish an international status for the state on the international stage. Any of them can be translated into strong political influence. Nonetheless, military strength remains the most prominent and effective for it is the title of the state and the symbol of it's power. Military strength is always seen behind a politicians actions as a possible option when all other means fail.

Military strength cannot be detached from the will to use it. The readiness to use it adds to it's strength and the lack of will to use it weakens it. The willingness of a state to use it's military weakens against a state that is much stronger than it or when the military strength of both states reaches problematic levels. This occurs when an arms race between them leads them to a point where they are able to destroy each other completely. In such a situation, the importance of the other state's strengths, such as, it's ideological and political ability and it's economic and diplomatic strength becomes apparent.

A state functions on the international scene to establish and protect it's interests. A state's interests outside of it's domain vary in number. Some of it's interests are ideological, such as creating an atmosphere conducive for the spread of it's ideology. Some are moralistic such as keeping it's status, dignity, and international position. Some of it's interests are materialistic, such as issues related to security like the need for strategic locations, raw materials, and markets to export it's surplus industrial and agricultural products.

Interests are of two types, vital and secondary. The vital interest is that for which the state is ready to engage in an immediate war. The vital interests increase and decrease proportionally to the strength and weakness of the state. A strong state has many vital interests and consequently, it's international relations and presence on the international stage increases. It is the interests of the state that dictate the state's relations with others, not the other way around. The size of the states' interests is set by the type and size of the state'. For example, a regional state's interests, concerns and relations are confined to a region and consequently it makes it's regional interests the sphere for it's political activities. A global state, however, organises it's interests all over the world and has concerns and relations in every corner of the globe, and consequently, the entire world is it's political stage.

What has to be clear is that understanding the international situation means to understand the international relations and their structure, the continuous competition among the various states for the position of leading state and effecting international politics. Consequently, understanding the stand of the world's leading state is of great importance to understand international politics as well as the international situation. In times of peace, the leading state is considered the one with the final word in the international situation. In such times, the second state is equal in it's political influence on the international situation as any other state. The influence other states have on the international situation results from their ability to influence the leading state. The influence a state can have on the leading state is directly proportional to the state's own strength as well as it's international strength and consequently that is the extent to which it can influence international politics. Nonetheless, and relatively speaking, the leading state is the most able to direct international politics to it's advantage and influence the international situation. It is due to the above that understanding every influential state on the international arena is the basis for understanding the international situation.

The struggle with the first state over it's position and constant competition among active states in order to influence international politics has existed since ancient times. In every period of history, there was a state that was viewed as the leading state. Sometimes there existed other states that competed with the leading state for it's position. This competition, however, did not manifest itself through political activities, but rather through military actions, such as wars and attacks to conquer states. This situation lasted until the mid-eighteenth century when international law evolved to become law and legislation. From that point onwards, political actions started to become an important aspect of international relations and in resolving international conflicts. Since then, political actions replaced military means in resolving disputes, curtailing the domination of the leading state and competing for it's position. Political actions carried out by states in general, states competing against the leading state, and the leading state in particular are based on what is called international norms and international law. As a matter of fact, these actions have become dependent on international law and legitimacy.

In order to understand the international situation and international politics there must exist guidelines explaining the political situation of every state and it's relationship with other world states, especially with the major states that influence the direction of events in the world. One should keep in mind however, the political plans of the countries and the styles used in their execution as well as the political manoeuvres performed by them. States engage in political actions for the purpose of fostering their national interests and establish their relations with others in accordance with these interests. The state that embraces a specific ideology and carries it to the world, makes the ideology an active component in it's international relations and specifies it's interests outside of it's domain. Therefore, it is mandatory that the Muslim *Ummah*, which is working to establish the Islamic state and carry the Da'wah to the world, familiarises itself with the states with respect to the ideas they embrace and whether they are ideological or not. The *Ummah* will then be in a position to know the factors that affect these state's international relations and interests, and trace back these relations in order to understand their hidden details and goals, so as to distinguish between what is a manoeuvre and what is not, the action and it's goals and be aware of the latest situation in terms of the international relations.

It must be clear, however, that the international situation does not remain static but varies. The position of each state does not remain the same from the international point of view, it goes through phases of strength or weakness, and of effectiveness or ineffectiveness. The relations between a given state and other states also differ and vary. Such changes demand the continuous political culturing of the *Ummah*. They also require the *Ummah* to continuously follow up and comprehend foreign politics in it's actual terms. Carrying the Islamic Da'wah is the determining factor and the controller of these politics.

These are the principles for understanding the international situation. Every politician must have information regarding the international situation and must follow up with it in order for him/her to have a clear view of things and be able to, through political analysis, pass judgement on every political event in a way where his/her judgement is close to the truth and reality. Political analysis is the method to judge any political event in any area in the world. It is dependent on understanding the political situation of that area or country and it's relation with international politics.

7

The International Community, it's Norms & Laws

To understand the reality of political actions and how these actions are executed from the international perspective one must have an understanding of the international norms and law. With regard to the international norms, they are as old as the states and entities. International norms are a group of rules which resulted from human relations in wartime as well as in peace. As a result of their observance by human groups over an extended period of time, these rules became international norms. This group of rules became permanent among states, and states started to voluntarily consider themselves committed to adhering to them, so they almost became a law. Such commitment is moral, not material and human groups adhered to them voluntarily and out of fear of public opinion. Whoever did not observe them was rebuffed by public opinion.

An example of an international norm is the norm of not fighting in the sacred months which existed amongst the Arabs prior to Islam. It was due to such an agreed upon norm that the Quraysh denounced the Messenger 鶏 when the expedition of Abdullah b. Jahsh killed Amru b. Al-Hadrami and took two Qurayshi men as prisoners and captured the trade caravan. Quraysh started spreading the propaganda that Muhammad 鶏 and his companions desecrated the sacred month, spilled people's blood, took their wealth and imprisoned other men. They agitated public opinion against him because he went against international norms.

Among the various communities, there existed well-known rules which were followed in times of both war and peace, such as, Messengers or ambassadors and war booty, among others. Some of these norms are general and observed by all human communities, such as, ambassadors or Messengers. Other norms are exclusive to certain communities. These norms evolved and developed according to the needs of states, emirates and entities, i.e. according to the needs of communities in their relations with each other. People judged on the observance of these international norms, to the public opinion, and scorned those who went against them. States used to adhere to these norms freely and willingly and for no other reason than a moral obligation. There was no material power to enforce them. Based on those norms, political actions were carried out by the various communities.

With regard to the so called International law, it was initiated to counter the Islamic state, represented by the then Ottoman state. The Ottoman state, being an Islamic state, fought against Europe and declared Jihad against the Christians of Europe and as a result conquered their lands one land after another. The state swept through Greece, Romania, Albania, Yugoslavia, Hungary and Austria, stopping at the gates of Vienna. It spread terror among all Christians in Europe. It was commonly held amongst the Christians that the Islamic army was undefeatable, and that Muslims care less for death when engaged in war because they believe that they will enter paradise if killed, that they believe in divine destiny (*Qadar*) and that each has a life span that none will go beyond (*Ajal*). Christians witnessed enough of the Muslims courage and awesome might to make them flee from them. This, in turn made conquering the lands and subjugating them to the Islamic authority easier. The Christians in Europe then were fiefdoms and feudal entities. They were fragmented states, each state was divided into fiefdoms, with each one governed by a feudal lord who shares with the king his power. This situation made it difficult for the king to force these feudal lords to fight and prevented him from protecting them from conquerors and representing them in foreign affairs, which made it easier for the Muslims to fight and conquer them.

The European states affairs remained in shambles until the middle ages, i.e. till the end of the sixteenth century. During the sixteenth century, European countries started to gather into one family, able to stand in the face of the Islamic state. The church controlled these countries and Christianity was the common element among them. The church attempted to form a Christian family that was composed of these states and started to organise the relations among them. This resulted in them formulating rules which they agreed upon to organise relations amongst themselves. This was the starting point for what was later called the International Law. Therefore, the basis of the formulation of International Law was when the Christian European countries, came together on the basis of the Christian bond, to confront the Islamic state which lead to the establishment of what is called the International Christian family. They agreed upon certain rules among themselves, such as, the equal rights of participating countries, and that all such countries share the same ideals and values. All these states, despite their different sectarian affiliations acknowledged the supreme spiritual authority of the Catholic Pope. These rules represented the nucleus of International law.

However, this consolidation of the Christian states was ineffective. The rules adopted could not unite them due to the presence of the feudal system that remained an obstacle preventing the individual states from becoming strong and from handling foreign affairs. The Church's control of these states turned them into it's subjects and stripped them of their sovereignty and independence. As a result, a struggle on two fronts took place; one was between the state and the feudal lords, and the other was between the state and the Church. The state emerged from both conflicts victorious by abolishing the feudal system and wiping out the church's authority from internal as well as external affairs. Nonetheless, the state remained Christian, and all that really happened was that the states relations with the Church were organised in such a way that emphasised the states independence.

Consequently, strong states emerged in Europe; but they remained unable to stand in the face of the Islamic state. This situation continued to exist until the mid seventeenth century i.e. till 1648. In that year, the Christian European states held the conference of Westphalia. In that conference they established the rules regulating the relations among the European Christian nations and organised the family of Christian countries against the Islamic state. When the conference established the traditional basis for the so-called International Law, it was not an international law for all states. Rather it was an international law for the Christian European states exclusively. It prohibited the Islamic state from joining the International family and it was not even subject to the law. Since then, what was called the International community came into existence. The International Community was composed of the various Christian states alike without differentiating between the kingship and

republican states or between the Catholic or Protestant states. It was
initially exclusive to the states of Western Europe but was later joined by
the rest of the Christian European states and at a later point in time,
non-European Christian nations. It remained prohibited for the Islamic
state to join until the second half of the nineteenth century when the
Islamic state had become weak and was known as the sick man of
Europe. At that point, the Islamic state applied for membership in the
International family but application was denied. The Ottoman state
strongly appealed the decision. As a condition for acceptance, severe
terms were placed upon it, such as removing Islam as a basis for it's
international relations and adopting some European laws. Only after
accepting and submitting to these terms and only after it accepted to
abandon it's identity as an Islamic state in international relations was it's
application approved. Consequently, it was admitted into the
International family in 1856. Thereafter, other non-Christian states were
admitted into the International family, such as Japan.

Thus the conference of Westphalia held in 1648 was considered as
the platform that launched the rules for International Law. Based on
these rules distinct political activities and collective international actions
came into existence. From amongst these rules, emerged two prominent
and dangerous ideas. The first was the idea of international balance of
power and the second was the idea of International conventions. With
regard to the international balance of power, it mandates that should
any country attempt to expand it's territory at the expense of another
country's account all other countries are to consolidate their efforts to
prevent it from expansion. Maintaining the international balance of
power is the guarantee for preventing the outbreak of war and for
establishing peace. As for the idea of International conventions, various
European states would convene to discuss their problems and affairs in
the light of European interests. This idea evolved to superpower
conferences to discuss the worlds affairs in the light of superpower
interests. Both ideas were the source of what the world faces in it's
attempt to remove the domination of the imperialists and major states.

This is the origin of International Law. It is what gave the superpowers
the pretext to intervene and control other states. It is the reference used
by these states in their political activities for executing their interests or
for competing with the leading state. These international rules have in

time been modified. This modification however is done in favour of the superpowers and for organising their interests. In other words, the division of the world's resources amongst them in a manner that does not lead to wars and armed conflicts. Modification of international relations changed the idea of conventions to an international organisation that is geared to keeping international security. Such modification did not change anything, for the superpowers continued to struggle over the spoils until the Second World War. Once the Second World War ended, the superpowers viewed the creation of an international organisation as the best way to organise their relations with each other. In the beginning, they formed the organisation from those who participated in the war, they then expanded it into an international organisation, open for all the states of the world. They organised international relations according to this organisation's convention. With this, international relations evolved from a convention of the superpowers who controlled the world in order to distribute the spoils amongst themselves and to prevent emergence of any new superpower, to an international organisation that organises relations amongst themselves and guarantees their domination. In addition, it evolved into an international organisation that acts as a global state, organising the affairs of the states of the world and controlling them.

These Christian states or Capitalist states did not leave the implementation of the traditional rules which evolved to be the International Law as a moral obligation as is the case with international norms and agreements. As a matter of fact nor did they make their implementation exclusively for those who committed themselves to them, rather the laws were enforced upon all states, whether they had committed to them or not.

Prior to the First World War, the Christian nations either individually or collectively made themselves the global policemen to enforce international law. Even after the establishment of the League of Nations followed by the United Nations, the Capitalist states considered themselves as the global policemen responsible for enforcing law and world order. This has had terrible consequences. One of the major causes of world misery has been the establishment of the international family and so called international law. Therefore this issue must be dealt with in order to rid the world from it and save it from misery.

The treatment for this problem is as follows: If there is to be an international group in the international community, it must not be compared with the regular society. In a regular society, there must exist an entity to settle disputes and remove acts of injustice, which means every society must have a state and an authority. There must exist a law that must be enforced upon the people. The international community, on the other hand, is made of human societies that have relations among them, not individuals with relations. Each group has the right of sovereignty and free will with no restriction or limitations. Any enforcement of certain laws on these groups or states means stripping them of their sovereignty. This is enslavement represented by imperialism, foreign control and compulsion. Stopping any group or state from carrying out it's own decisions is effectively tying it hands and crippling it.

Therefore, no power should dominate states or act as an authority over them as that means domination by a single group. In other words, it is not correct for the international community to become a group with an authority that has the right to take care of it's affairs. Thus, no global entity should exist or be allowed to exist with authority over several human groups. Rather, the human groups must continue as entities, each has it's own structure, sovereignty and will. If it was necessary to establish an international community of these entities, it should not be a global state. Furthermore, this community must be established by those who choose to be members in it. It should not be initiated by a specific state carrying specific concepts or by specific states that enjoy a power superior to other's powers, nor should it be established as a global state. Instead, the international community should be formed by all those who wish to form it, regardless of their concepts, strengths and influence. All states that did not participate in initiating the group should have the full choice to join the international group at any time and to enjoy the same rights and duties the founders have. Every state should feel free to dismember itself from the international group at any time they wish. Decisions and resolutions should not be enforced upon anyone by force. Only then can it truly be called an International group. And only then, would it not be a specific international family falsely called the international family, not a global state falsely called the UN.

The position that should be taken in reference to the Security Council and the UN institutions is that work should be undertaken to abolish them. They should be replaced with a new international organisation that the superpowers have no control or authority over and which does not act as a global state. The new organisation should be an international entity that removes injustice and helps those who are oppressed, to dominate injustice, and works to spread justice amongst mankind. Such goals would be achieved through the moral status it enjoys and the international public opinion that supports it, and respects and trusts it for it would be an organisation that serves the interests of no particular state or states, but serves all mankind. This would be similar to the covenant of *Fudul* (favours) held prior to the mission of Muhammad 鐮 and attended by Allah's Messenger before he became a Messenger 鐮. After he became a Messenger 鐮, he said about it: **I witnessed a covenant in the tribe of Abdullah b. Jadaan that I liked more than the red (expensive) camels. If I were invited to it after Islam, I would have accepted it.** This organisation would serve as a platform to present creeds and ideas pertaining to life for discussions where the true idea of them should be taken as the thought and creed of the world.

As for international law and it's forced implementation upon the people, it should not exist or be allowed to exist. This is because law is the order of the one in authority and there is no global state or authority. Therefore there should not exist a global state that has authority over all states because it is impossible. Claiming it's existence means the outbreak of wars and bloody conflicts, and because of this there should not be a global authority or state. Consequently, there should not be an international law, even in theory. With regard to implementing international law upon the people by force, it should not occur, because enforcing the law, if done by a global authority, i.e. by a global state, is impossible, for there is no such state. If enforcement of the law is carried out by two or more leading states it is considered aggression, not enforcement of law, because if one of the states that enforces the law did not abide by the law, the other states will not be able to subject it to the law, as that would mean war. Also if the two states or all the states disobey the law, who is to enforce it upon them? No-one. Therefore, when the strong state enforces the law on the small or weak states, it is in reality aggression and not the implementation of International Law. Thus, it becomes apparent that implementing the law on all nations is incorrect and enforcing such a law is nothing but aggression.

Based on the above, there should not be an international law, and as a matter of fact, it cannot exist practically. What should exist is merely agreements among nations and certain norms they abide by pertaining to these agreements, as well as relations of war and peace among different communities. Therefore, if we are to form an international group, it should have an administrative law only. It's function would be to look into international norms, and violations of them. Such norms would include norms pertaining to international treaties as far as their signature, implementation and nullification, etc.

This international norm should only be implemented by moral obligation and the pressure of public opinion, and not by force. The member states in the international group would not consider a rule to be an international norm until it is has been verified that it has become a norm. Then, there would be no reason to use force to implement it for they are convinced that this norm should be followed. Furthermore, the power of the general public opinion against the state which violates the norm, obliges such a state willingly and by itself, more than the external physical force. Human communities fear being looked down upon for going against the public norm more than physical force. Therefore, implementing the group's resolution should be left to public opinion and moral obligation. This would be the method for implementing the community resolutions.

8
Political Thinking

Political thinking differs completely from legislative thinking even though it is true that both are of the same type. Because legislative thinking is for solving people's problems and political thinking is for looking after people's affairs. Nevertheless, there is a difference between them. Political thinking also contradicts the literary thinking completely for literary thinking is concerned with languages and the pleasure gained from using words and phrases, where enjoyment is attained when meanings are expressed in word forms presented in literary style. As for the intellectual way of thinking and it's similarity to the political way of thinking, it is detailed. If political thinking is exercised in political science and research texts, then it is very similar to the intellectual way of thinking. As a matter of fact, they are almost the same type. With regard to intellectual thinking it requires previous information that is on the same level of thought under such previous information, while not necessarily being of the same type, it must be related to it. Political thinking, on the other hand not only requires previous information on the level of thought but it also requires the previous information to be on the same topic. It is not sufficient for the previous information here to be just related to, or similar to, or even information that can explain it. Therefore, thinking about political texts is the same as thinking about intellectual texts.

In the case of political thinking, it is about news and events, and deals with connecting events with each other, it differs from all types of thinking. It does not follow any of it's rules. As a matter of fact, it is not governed by any rule. That is why it is the highest and most difficult type of thinking. As for being the highest type of thinking, it is because it is thinking of things and events and of all types of thinking. Therefore it is the highest of them all. It is true that the intellectual basis upon which ideas are based and from which solutions emanate is the highest form of thinking. But this basis itself is political thinking and a political thought. If it is not political thought and thinking, it is not a correct basis nor is it fit to be one. So, when we say that political thought is the highest form of thinking it includes the intellectual basis i.e. that which is fit to be an intellectual basis. As for being the most difficult type of thinking, it is due to the absence of a rule for it, upon which it is built and measured. That is why it confuses the thinker making him initially subject to many errors and prey to erroneous impressions and mistakes. Unless the person gains political experience and stays alert and follows up all daily events, it will be difficult for him to master political thinking. Therefore, political thinking related to news and events is distinguished from all forms of thinking and has an edge on all of them.

Thinking about political texts includes thinking about texts of political sciences and research, but true political thinking is that which is concerned with the text of the news and events. Therefore the manner in which news is presented is the true political texts. If a person wants to exercise political thinking, he should do it upon news texts, concentrating on the manner in which it is presented and understanding such texts.

This is what is considered political thinking, not thinking about political science and research. Thinking about political science and research gives information, exactly as thinking about intellectual texts gives deep or enlightened thought, but it does not make the thinker a politician. It merely makes the person knowledgeable of politics, meaning political study. Such a person would be a good teacher but not a politician. This is because a politician is the one who understands news and events with their indications. He would then attain the type of knowledge that would enable him to act whether he has knowledge of political science and research or not. It is true that political sciences and research help to understand news and events, however it is only limited to helping in sorting out information, when it comes to connecting information, hence, it is not a condition for political thinking.

Unfortunately, since the emergence of the idea of detaching religion from state and the concept of compromise has dominated secularists, the

West i.e. Europe and America have had the monopoly in producing literature and writing books on political science. The western literature has been written based on it's viewpoint of life, the compromise solution and on formalities that advocate compromise thought that was founded to make conciliation and defuse conflicts. Upon the emergence of the communist ideology and when Russia, the communist state, embraced it, one became hopeful that political science on a fixed basis other than that of compromise would emerge.

Unfortunately, Russia continued to follow the West. Consequently, political sciences and political studies continued on the same course, with some differences in superficial issues only. From the above, one can say that existing political study available currently is questionable in validity. Political science is similar to so called psychology which is based on guesswork and probability, in addition to being based on the concept of compromise. Thus, when analysing the texts of these sciences and studies one must be alert to these ideas, and care must be taken not to be drawn to their erroneous ideas, for they contain ideas contrary to reality and studies that are completely false. It is preferable to deal with these studies as Western legislation where it should not be read for it contains legislative aspects rather than politics such as the discussion of ruling systems. Since they are types of intellectual studies and contain political aspects, then there is no harm to read and study them but we must be cautious and take care.

An example of what is discussed in Western political studies is the Western concept of leadership. According to the West, leadership is pluralistic, represented by ministers. The East too, adopted this concept, although it was presented in a different form and called pluralistic leadership. This is contrary to reality as well as based on the concept of compromise. The tyrant kings in Europe, who were individuals, caused the people to become discontent with their tyranny, and they attributed this tyranny to the individual leadership. As a result of this they said that leadership should belong to the people, and not to the individual. The idea was embodied in the formation of a cabinet of ministers. This was a compromise solution. This is because the cabinet is not the people nor is it elected by the people. The Prime Minister too is the one who leads the ministers and thus leadership is not left to the people or the individual. Rather, leadership is left for the Prime Minister and not the cabinet ministers. Therefore, this system is a compromise leadership solution between the individual and the people. It is clear that it does not resolve the issue of leadership but is a solution that pleases both parties. Moreover, historically speaking, leadership has remained individualistic in the various democratic systems. In reality, it is either exercised by the head of state such as the President of the republic or the Prime Minister himself. Therefore, leadership in reality is always individualistic. It is not possible to make leadership pluralistic at all. Even if it is made pluralistic or so called, the manner that ruling is executed makes leadership individualistic, for it cannot be but that.

For the West, sovereignty is given to the people; it is the people who legislate rules and it is the people who have the will and the decision. Thus, the people share the power to legislate and rule so they say that sovereignty belongs to the people who legislate and hence, they gave the power to legislate to an elected council which actually does legislate. The one who legislates is effectively the ruler, and the cabinet of ministers or the President of the republic is the one who rules. While the Prime Minister or the President is directly elected by the people or agreed upon by their representatives, it does not mean that the people actually rule. The people simply choose the ruler and thus it is a compromise solution. Furthermore, they declare that supremacy is to the law, and consider good ruling to be that which guarantees the supremacy of the law. Therefore, this system is a compromise solution and contains contradictions within it, moreover, the reality of ruling is not as stated.

The only correct and valid ruling system is that where the people choose their ruler and where sovereignty belongs to the law. Sovereignty shouldn't belong to the people nor should the ruling. For the West, ruling is something that should not be mixed with sentimental and religious affairs. In their view, the authority of the church is different from that of the state, and that sentimental actions such as charitable deeds, caring for the poor, taking care of the sick and the like are not the state's responsibility. This is based on the idea of the detachment of religion from the state, which is a solution based on compromise which conflicts with reality. This idea emerged from the time that tyrant kings used to be in control of the church. They cared not for the wounded, the sick, the poor and the like which is why people rebelled. As a result, they arrived at a compromise that led to the detachment of church from state and hence taking away the sentimental actions from the state's responsibility. Hence, the authority of the state became separate from that of the church, and charitable associations and the association of the Red Cross and it's like came into being.

The truth of the matter however is that ruling is fostering of the affairs of the people. Religion and sentimental actions are both of the affairs. This is why the state oversees churches, charitable and Red Cross type associations in an implicit manner. Hence, this theory of ruling contradicts with reality, since officially ruling is detached from these other aspects.

Above are three examples that serve as an example of the fallacy of the political thoughts contained in the political studies of the West. This fallacy is not only with the political ideas related to the system but also with the political studies concerned with matters and events. While these ideas and studies contain some truth in certain matters, they are filled with things that contradict reality and erroneous ideas. For example, British policy is described as being based on three points: England's relationship with America, England's relationship with Europe and finally it's relationship with the ex-colonies that became independent i.e. Commonwealth countries. These policy descriptions are true, because it is a description of reality for which fallacy cannot occur. But when they speak of British policy with regard to it's behaviour in treaties, it's position toward it's allies or enemies, the manner it views people's and nations, is not only filled with fallacies but is also in contradiction with reality. This fallacy exists whenever they describe a nation's position, Western or otherwise, historically or contemporarily, and whether describing on-going events or not. They are extremely skilled in leading people astray, fabricating events and falsifying facts. Therefore, thinking about political science and studies of any type must be done with extreme alertness and caution.

With regard to political thinking about events and incidents it is the type of thinking that is worthy of being described as political by the full meaning of the word. Since it is what makes the thinker a politician. For this type of thinking to take place, it requires primarily 5 points to exist at the same time:

(1) It requires keeping up with (pursuance) of all events and incidents

taking place in the world. News differs with respect to it's importance and with regard to the occurrence due to being coincidental or intentional, reporting the news and the manner of reporting it in terms of brevity or elaboration. With practice, keeping up with the news will no longer include all news but only that which must be known in the chain of knowledge.

(2) It requires information whether primary or abridged, concerning the essence of the incidents and events i.e. the significance of the news whether the news is geographical, historical, intellectual, political etc. In other words, the information should enable the person to know the reality of the incident i.e. the true meaning of the news.

(3) Events should not be detached from their circumstances nor should they be generalised. Absolutism, generalisations and overall analogy are the disease of understanding events and incidents i.e. the problem in understanding news. The incident or the event must be studied with it's circumstances, i.e. as one unit that is inseparable. Thus, it should not be compared to a similar one by generalisation nor should a general analogy be used to compare a similar incident with it. A single incident must be studied alone, and judgement should be passed over it alone.

(4) Differentiating between the events and the incident by completely scrutinising them. Hence, knowledge of the source of the news, place where the event occurred, time of it's occurrence, circumstances of occurrence, and the purpose of it's existence is a must. In addition, one should bear in mind whether the news was brief or detailed, true or false. This is all included in scrutinising the news. Such scrutiny is what produces differentiation between truth and falsehood. The more comprehensive and deep the scrutiny the better the differentiation. Without differentiating the news, one can not accept an incident or event because one would become prey to error or being led astray. That is why differentiation is an important factor in accepting the news or even listening to it.

(5) Connecting the news with other information, especially other news. Such connection leads us to being closer to the correct judgement on news. If the news is connected with something other than what it

should be linked with, errors will definitely occur, even deception. Examples of this include if news is related to local politics or is linked with international politics or visa versa; or if news related to the economy is connected with economics while it is a political event, even though it is related to the economy; or if news which is related to Germany is connected to German politics while it is in fact related to America; then error even deception will occur. Therefore linking the news to that which it is related to is of extreme importance. Furthermore, this connection must be done in the correct fashion, in other words, connecting the news must be for the purpose of understanding and comprehension, not for mere knowledge, i.e. words making the connection must be for the sake of action not information.

All the above five points must exist together for thinking on the political texts to take place i.e. for political thinking to exist. It should not be said that these points are numerous and difficult to achieve because achieving these points is not hard, all that is required is an overall knowledge, not a vast detailed understanding. This would come gradually with time, not at once, and it comes with pursuance of the news, not through study and scientific research. While it is true that study and scientific research further enhances one's ability, it is not a requirement for political thinking nor for politicians but is secondary and complimentary.

The most important of the above five points is following up of events (pursuance), and once it exists, the remaining points come naturally. Thus, the basic tenet in political thinking is the pursuance. Once it exists, political thinking will exist naturally.

Consequently, while political thinking is difficult and complicated, it lies within the ability of every person regardless of his level of thinking and knowledge. Whether the person is of average ability or a genius, he is able to have political thinking and to be a politician. This is due to the fact that political thinking does not require a certain level of intelligence or a certain degree of knowledge. It merely requires pursuance of the events and current incidents i.e. keeping up with the news, for once the pursuance exists, political thinking will exist. Pursuance of the news, however, must be continuous, not interrupted because events and current incidents are connected much like the links of a chain. If one piece is missing, the chain is disconnected i.e. the link will be missing. As a result, a person becomes unable to connect pieces of news together and to understand it. Therefore, maintaining the link is necessary in political thinking. In other words, the continuous pursuance of the news is a fundamental condition for political thinking.

Political thinking is not exclusive to individuals. It exists on the level of groups as well as individuals i.e. it can exist in people and nations. It is unlike literary or legislative thinking which may only be present in individuals and are thus individualistic, lies beyond the capability of groups. Political thinking on the other hand is individualistic as well as collective and thus it exists in individuals, such as, politicians and rulers as well as in peoples and nations. As a matter of fact, it is not sufficient for it to exist among individuals, rather it must be present among peoples and nations. Without it being present among the masses, the proper way of governing and revival will not take place, nor will a people, or a nation be able to carry the message to mankind.

Hence, it is vital that political thinking exists in the masses of people and nation. This is because authority belongs to the people or the *Ummah*. No one can acquire it unless it is given to him by the people of the *Ummah*. If it is taken by force, it will only be temporary. Sooner or later, the *Ummah* will decide either to give it to the person who took it by force or to insist on taking it back from him, which will consequently lead to the removal of the regime. Since, authority belongs to the people or the *Ummah*, the *Ummah* or the people have to be capable of political thinking. Therefore, political thinking is a necessity for the *Ummah* more than the rulers and is more than simply establishing it.

Consequently, it is imperative that the *Ummah* or the people are cultured politically and that they possess political thinking. i.e. it is of paramount importance that the *Ummah* is provided with political information and news. Listening to political reports has to be made easy for her, but in a natural way and not in a manner that is contrived. She has to be given the correct political culture and the honest news so that she does not fall prey to deception. Accordingly, politics and political thinking is that which generate life in the *Ummah* i.e. politics is that which the *Ummah* lives by, and without which the *Ummah* will be a lifeless corpse that has no movement or growth.

However, the error that is made in understanding politics or the misguidance that takes place in understanding politics only comes when one thinks about the political texts in the same manner as thinking about other literary, intellectual and legislative texts. Thus, he thinks about the words and phrases for example and these words and phrases are understood as they are. Or, he thinks about the meanings contained by these words and phrases and these meanings are understood as they are. Or he thinks about the implications of these words and phrases and these implications are understood. This is where the mistake occurs, because thinking about political texts differs completely from thinking about any other text. The mistake and danger in political thinking comes solely from a failure to differentiate between political texts and other types of texts. Thus, with political texts, their meanings may be present within or outside the texts, or they may be present in the wording of the terms and phrases, as in treaties or in official statements. Or they may be in the meaning and not in the wording. And they may be in the implications and not in the meanings or words. Or it might be behind the meanings, words and implications. Indeed, it might contradict them or be completely opposite to them. When someone does not distinguish between what the text means and that which is contained in the text or is external to it, then he has not understood the text at all and he is liable to fall prey to mistakes or deceptions in thinking about the political text.

Furthermore, one of the most dangerous matters for political thinking is it's detachment or disassociation, generalisation and allowing the comprehensive analogy into the thinking. The political texts cannot be detached from their circumstances in any way whatsoever, as the circumstances are a part of the political text. Neither is it correct at all to generalise or allow any comprehensive analogy or even analogy for that matter. In addition to the circumstances being part of the text, it is a text regarding a specific incident or event. Thus, the text is taken for that event only and none other. It is not generalised with anything else and nor is any comparison made with it, whether broad or literal. Rather the text should be taken for that event and only that event. This is why detachment, generalisation and analogy - whether comprehensive or literal - constitute a dangerous error and misguidance for political thinking. An official might make a statement from which something is understood and then he might make the same or another statement from which something else is understood. It may differ or contradict the initial understanding. An official may make a statement about something real, i.e. a statement that is true, but it is understood as a lie by which deception is intended. Or he might make a false statement which is understood to be true, and it is taken to mean what he intended. While the lie in it is that he gave it to conceal or cover up with the lie. An action may be taken in accordance with the statement or an action may be taken contrary to the statement. Thus, it is the circumstances and surrounding conditions that throw light on the statement revealing it's meaning, and not the political text itself. Therefore, political thinking will not even come close to being correct unless it is done in this manner. i.e. unless each event is taken individually and free from generalisation and analogy.

The Muslim *Ummah* has suffered many misfortunes and calamities due to poor political thinking. The Ottoman state for example, when fought by Europe in the 19th century, was subjected more to political actions than military actions. Even though military actions did take place, they were used to assist the political actions. For instance, what was called the Balkan question, was a problem created by Western states merely through statements. They declared that the Balkan nations should be liberated from the Ottomans i.e. from the Muslims. However, they did not mean that they would fight the Ottoman state, rather they relied on inciting unrest and disturbances in the Balkans. Thus, they brought the idea of nationalism and liberation. The peoples of the Balkans adopted it and started revolts. The Ottoman state undertook military operations against these uprisings thereby complying with the stance of the other nations and attempted to appease these nations even though they were supporting the revolts and implied to the Ottomans otherwise. They were the ones who made them remain preoccupied with the revolts in order that their power wore out rather than suppressing these revolts. Thus, as a result of the Ottoman state's mistakes and misguidance in political thinking the Balkans were lost. Furthermore, in it's own house, the state became afflicted by the concept of nationalism until it destroyed her completely.

Poor political thinking destroys peoples and nations, it demolishes states or weakens them. It is that which stands as an obstacle between peoples and emancipation from the control of colonialism. It stands between declined nations and their revival. Therefore, thinking about political statements is of immense importance and it's results can be disastrous or great, and the results of making a mistake or being misguided can be destructive. Consequently, it is imperative that the attention given to political thinking is of the first order, which surpasses the attention given to any other type of thinking. This is because political thinking is indispensable for peoples and indispensable for life.

Even though political thinking is one of the most difficult and highest types of thought, it is not enough that only individuals use it. Individuals have no value however many they may be, and however sound or ingenious their thinking may be. If deception in political thinking gained ground (spread) in peoples and nations, the seriousness of the individuals will not avail towards it. The seriousness of people has no value in political thinking whatever their number and seriousness in thinking. For if misguidance gained ground in a nation or people then it's current will sweep everything away. The nation or people will find themselves a target for such misguidance. The nation or people and with them it's geniuses become an easy prey for enemies to devour. The success of Mustafa Kamal in destroying the Islamic state and eliminating the Khilafah at the beginning of the twentieth century, and the success of Jamal 'Abd al-Nasir in the fifties and sixties from this century, in preventing the liberation of the Arabs when at the end of the 1st World War they were ready for liberation; are live examples of poor political thinking which overwhelms peoples and nations. The most brilliant of geniuses would be of no help, as long as they remain as individuals, even if their numbers were to reach into the thousands. Therefore, poor political thinking does not constitute a danger for individuals but is a danger for peoples and nations. From here, the attention given by peoples and nations to political thinking must be an attention that surpasses everything else. It is correct that when political thinking exists in individuals and they have the correct method then they can generate political thinking that will stand in the face of the enemy and expose their deception. But this will only happen when the thinking of those individuals is transferred to the people or nation. When the people possess political thinking in the same way as the individuals, and when it moves to being the thinking of nations and not the thinking of individuals, then those individuals become part of the nation and not individuals. The entire nation becomes an intellectual nation and not just individuals within it. If the individual thinking does not develop into a collective thinking, and the thinking of the individuals does not become the thinking of a nation but rather remains the thinking of individuals, then such thinking, and those individuals, would be of no value. The political thinking of individuals, whatever their number and their ingenuity, is not strong enough to stand in the face of the enemy and in the face of their deception. What can stand up to them is the thinking of people and nations i.e. the political thinking possessed by the peoples and nations.

It is correct that geniuses are ordinary people, i.e they are like the rest of the people. In their lives they are no different from any other ordinary human being. The people look at those individuals from an ordinary perspective, their genius is not seen, felt or sensed. That is why when their ingenuity is set in motion and they are productive, in the first instance one cannot observe any distinguishing features or realise from their output any excellence or genius. Even though they are learned, they are like many other educated people. And even if they are intelligent, they are like many other intelligent people. When attention is given to their thoughts, it is given via other individuals, who accept their contribution in order to be like them or so that this thinking will assist their elevation in their society and circles, or to adopt it as a means to realise personal aspirations or selfish aims. If this continues, the thinking will not transfer to the groups. It will remain individualistic, however many individuals adopt this thought, even if the thinking is unique and it is accepted by anyone who tastes it and comes to know of it. This is why, for political thinking to be beneficial and to be able to stand up to and face the enemy, it is essential that it develops into a collective thinking and comes out from the snail shell of individualism and from the cocoon of isolation. When it changes to a collective thinking and transfers to the people or nation, then the power that faces the enemy exists, and so does the resilient seed from which the tree of revival will grow.

It is the collective thinking and not the individual thinking which is the most beneficial form of political thinking, i.e. it is the thinking of the people and the nation and not the thinking of individuals even if they were geniuses. It is essential to train and instruct the *Ummah* in the political thinking until political thinking becomes the thinking of the *Ummah* and not merely the thinking of individuals.

This is political thinking. It is the thinking re: the political sciences and political studies, and thinking re: the political events and political incidents. As for the first (type of) thinking, it has no value, it is no more than mere knowledge of ideas. As for political thinking, it is of benefit and use and has tremendous effect and great influence. Therefore, even though political thinking is allowed in political sciences and political studies, it has benefit for the individual scholars of politics. Thinking of the incidents and events is an obligation of sufficiency (Wajib 'ala al-kifaya) especially for those people who possess this type of thinking whether they are educated or uneducated.

9
Political Awareness

The Islamic state is an ideological state. It's main function is to carry the Islamic call to the world. Therefore, it must have international standing and be able to influence international relations. Consequently, the political concepts that are carried by politicians must be those related to international politics. They must not have concepts linked to regional or local politics alone. In other words, the politicians, being Muslims, must carry political concepts from an international angle and not from a local or regional angle alone. Therefore, as their state is an Islamic state, they have no choice but to enjoy complete political awareness. So, as Muslims, and as their state is the Islamic state, whose fundamental function is to carry the Islamic call to the world, it is mandatory for them to possess not only political awareness but that this awareness must be complete.

Political awareness does not only mean awareness of political and international situations, political events, or simply keeping up with international politics and actions, although these are required for it to be complete, but Political awareness means viewing the world from a particular angle. For Muslims, the particular angle is the Islamic Aqeedah, namely *La Ilaha illa Allah Muhammadur Rasoolullah*. Allah's Messenger ﷺ said: **"I was commanded to fight the people until they say La Ilaha ill Allah, Muhammadur Rasoolullah. If they say it, they will secure from me their blood and wealth except for what is rightfully due"**. This is political awareness, viewing the world without a particular angle is shallowness, and not political awareness. Furthermore restricting oneself to the local or regional domain is frivolity, and not political awareness. Political awareness cannot be achieved unless two elements are present; the entire world must be the domain of ones view and secondly this view must emanate from a particular angle, whether this angle is a specific ideology, thought, benefit or anything else.

This is the reality of political awareness. Naturally for the Muslim, the particular angle is the Islamic Aqeedah. Since this is the reality of political awareness, it becomes mandatory on the politician to engage in struggle to formulate a specific concept about life for man as a man in every place. Carrying this concept is the foremost responsibility to be carried on the politically aware person's shoulders. For him there will be no rest until he has exerted his utmost in establishing it.

The politically aware person must engage in struggle against all the (intellectual) trends that contradict his trend, and against concepts that contradict his concepts. At the time when he struggles to concentrate his concepts and establish deeply his trend, he moves in two directions at the same time. These two movements are inseparable in the struggle, for they are but one. He destroys and builds at the same time. He removes the darkness and brings light, and acts as a fire that burns corruption and a light that lightens the path of guidance. Therefore, he moves to establish his concept and direction, uses his ideas in addressing actual events, and remains far from separating events from their circumstance (abstraction) and from logic. He also struggles in all directions, dealing with opposing concepts about life as well as the deep rooted concepts that go back to the declined eras. In addition, he engages in struggle against the misleading influence spread by the enemies regarding thoughts and objects, and summarising the noble ideals and ambitious goals to partial goals and temporary achievements. Therefore, he struggles on two fronts: internal and external and in two directions: destroying and building, and he works on two levels: political and thinking. In short, he involves himself in life's affairs in it's most high and noble field.

As a result, the confrontation of those with awareness against issues when they come in contact with reality, the people and life's problems is inevitable. This confrontation will take place on the internal local front as well as on the international level. In such a confrontation, they make the message they carry, and the particular angle they have, according to the concept they carry, the basis, the criterion and the goal they seek and struggle for. However, since he has a particular angle and specific tastes and inclinations, whether natural or ideological, he might colour the facts according to his desires, interpret the thoughts the way he wants, and understand the news according to the result which he wants to reach.

Therefore, he must be careful lest his inclinations influence his view of the news. The selfishness of ones wishes, for a personal or ideological matter might make the person falsely interpret the news, or add to it that which makes the observer think of it as true when it is false, or as false when it is true. Therefore, the aware person must be sure of the speech that is said and actions that are being performed.

With regard to events, whether objects or events, he must understand them based on the senses and feels of them with logic as they are and not as one would like them to be. As for ideas, they must be understood in the context of their reality, so one must view the reality that is being expressed by the thought. He must then understand the thought in accordance with it's own reality, not in accordance with his wishes. Although, it is true that the expression at hand may be metaphoric or alluded to or a sentence that must be understood as a whole, not selected words. This however, should not prevent him from seeing the reality which the expression indicates according to the language.

The politically aware person must be on the side of the truth, in accordance with his point of view which he has adopted with certainty. He must see the facts as they are, in accordance with his sensory and intellectual vision. As a result of this, his awareness becomes complete since the tools needed to think are used. Nonetheless, his comprehension, perception, and vision must all be based on the unique angle from which he views the world.

A question related to this may arise; that is, how can a politically aware person be objective and see the facts as they are while he views the world from a specific angle? This question arises, only due to the shallow study of things. If a person studies things deeply, such a question does not arise. This is because there is a difference between the reality of things and passing a judgement on them. The reality of a thing is not subject to disagreement among people. If reality is related to eyesight, then anyone who is able to see, will be able to see the thing as it is, unless he is cheated or deceived. If reality is related to senses, then anyone who is able to sense an object, be it by taste, to sense it's sweetness and bitterness, or by touching, to sense it's softness and texture, or by hearing to sense sounds and noises, or by smelling e.g. perfumes, is capable of knowing the reality of the object. Therefore, objects are sensed by people as they are, regardless of their variations. However, passing judgement on things is what people disagree on. While looking at objects and actions from a specific angle is related to passing judgements on objects and actions, seeing facts as they are, is related to the senses and comprehension. Therefore, the person must see the facts as they are and stay on the side of the truth. Also, a person must look at the world, events and objects, from a specific angle.

With regard to the relationship of the above mentioned subject to international politics, studying some examples, shows how monitoring the political events is done from a particular angle. To demonstrate this point, examples from the political life of the Messenger ﷺ, the political events from the mid centuries and some examples from contemporary politics are presented.

The Messenger's specific angle meant that he viewed the world in order to spread the Da'wah. Since Quraysh were the super power in the peninsula and were the spearhead of *Kufr* in confronting the Da'wah, he restricted the political and military actions to them. So, he used to send his spies to keep abreast of their activities, attacked their trade and engaged in war with them. As for the other states i.e. the tribes, he accepted their neutrality. Hence, his political and military actions emerged from viewing the world from a specific angle. When the Messenger found that the tribe of Khaybar were negotiating with Quraysh to form an alliance in order to attack Medina and finish off Muhammad, ﷺ and hence demolish Islam, he determined the aspect of work. He ﷺ decided to conclude a truce or peace treaty with Quraysh, thereby enabling him to wipe out Khaybar. From this specific angle, he followed a policy of peace as a basis for his future activities. Thus, he went for Umrah, accepted the rejection of Quraysh, showed leniency towards the stubbornness of Quraysh, and disagreed with his companions, and performed other actions, all in accordance with his policy of peace. His view of political activities with the enemy which he focused his attention on was based on a specific angle, and was shaped according to what was required by this specific angle.

The above are two examples of the Messenger's actions. One of them was general, wherein he concentrated on a major state that was the most powerful of his enemies, from a specific angle. The second was specific, wherein he focused on a specific goal, from a specific angle and based on this, he undertook certain political and military actions. These examples show how viewing political events from a specific angle dominate actions and activities. It also shows that without this view that is based on a particular angle, actions will have no meaning.

The Superpowers, after the Berlin Conference, set about stripping the property of the Islamic state, i.e. the Ottoman state, rather than destroying it as their specific angle, though they had discussed both options. They agreed on the second option, which is the destruction of the state, but did not make it the specific angle in their international activities. As a result, they shaped all their political activities in accordance with this angle and entered into a political conflict with it that lasted for more than a century. While it is true that this political struggle ended with the destruction of the Islamic state, thereby finishing it off, this was not the specific angle these states viewed events and political activities from. Instead the specific angle which they adopted dominated their policies and perception of the political activities.

America, after the Second World War, stated that the world was but a corporation, and therefore should be under her control. She used this statement as her specific angle from which to view the world. As a result, she shaped her actions accordingly, and viewed political events in the world from this angle. It was this view that is based on this angle, that made her agree, to ally herself with the Soviet Union and made her oppose England and France. This is how the view based on a specific angle affects the political activities in the world. This angle may be general such as spreading the Da'wah as the basis for foreign affairs, i.e. the specific angle that the world is viewed from. This angle may also be specific, such as restricting animosity to a specific state that can be defeated enabling the state to then move to the world. This angle may be more specific such as engaging in a certain political battle in order to give other states a sample of our political capabilities. Applying the view from a specific angle to activities is an easy matter. It requires only the actual engagement in politics. As a matter of fact, in order to understand it, it is sufficient to examine political events in depth. Thus, it is clear that keeping up with politics and understanding political concepts must lead to political awareness. It is also clear that political awareness is not only essential for political work but a must to influence political events.

As political awareness of the super powers has become self evident and keeping up with international politics has become the daily bread for politicians, it is mandatory for the Muslim *Ummah*, the sons of the Islamic state, to consider political awareness as the most important political concept they carry. It should be the basis of their engagement in political activities. They should strive to make it prevail amongst the people and be self-evident in the society. They must make it the daily bread for their politicians. This is because their greatest task and principal responsibility is to carry the Islamic Da'wah to the world and spread guidance among the people. This cannot be achieved unless they are politicians, viewing the world from a specific angle, and unless they possess a complete political awareness.

In order for political awareness not to appear as unachievable except by the intelligent and the educated, the *Ummah* must know that it is not only very easy, but within easy reach even to the unlettered and the ordinary masses. The *Ummah* must know that political awareness does not mean a comprehensive knowledge of all world political events or Islam in it's totality, or what should be used as a specific angle from which to view the world. It means to view the entire world, irrespective of the knowledge and that this view should be based on a specific angle. What matters is the universal view even if it was one political action and that this view is based on one defined and particular angle. The mere presence of a view of the world from a particular angle is enough to indicate political awareness.

It is true that political awareness varies in strength and weakness due to the variation of knowledge about the world and political events, as well as knowledge of the particular angle. Nonetheless, it is political awareness and it leads to the same result, regardless of the variation. That result is to avoid superficiality in politics and rise above shallowness in viewing matters.

Therefore, political awareness is not exclusive to politicians and intellectuals nor should it be. It is inclusive to everyone and must be so. It is possible for it to exist amongst the unlettered and the general public as amongst the scholars and the educated. As a matter of fact it must be generated amongst the *Ummah* at large, even if general. This is because the *Ummah* is the soil out of which men grow and in order to develop men, account the rulers, evaluate men, and face foreign threats with true awareness, this soil must be one of political awareness.

The method to establish political awareness in individuals and the *Ummah* is via political culturing in the political sense. This culturing may be done with the Islamic ideas, and rules and must not be presented as if they were mere abstract theories. Rather, they should relate them to the events and incidents. Also the individual Muslim and the *Ummah* at large must keep up with the political events, not as reporters to merely be aware of the news events nor as academics in order to accumulate information. Rather it should be done to view events from the specific angle in order to judge them and to connect them with other events and ideas or with the political actions occurring.

Such political culturing with the ideology and politics is the method to create political awareness in the *Ummah* as well as in individuals. Also, political culturing is what makes the Muslim *Ummah* engage in it's most fundamental job, namely carrying the Da'wah to the world and spreading the guidance to mankind.

Thus, political culturing is the method to create political awareness in the *Ummah* and individuals. Consequently, there is a dire need to politically culture the *Ummah* to the maximum, for it is what creates political awareness in the *Ummah* and makes it develop politicians with initiative in great numbers.

10
Political Struggle

Any society is shaped according to the existing relations among it's people. These relations are regulated by specific thoughts and rules which the state executes upon the people. If corruption occurs in these relations or in the state that looks after the people's affairs, then the society is corrupted and consequently must be reformed. Islam has specified the method used to correct the corruption of the society as well as the corruption of the state, namely enjoining the good (*Ma'aroof*) and forbidding the evil (*Munkar*) with regard to reforming the society, and taking the rulers to task re: the corruption of the state.

What is called "political struggle" is itself enjoining the good and forbidding the evil and accounting the rulers. Therefore, engaging in political struggle is an obligation upon Muslims. Allah ﷻ says:

$$\text{وَلْتَكُنْ مِنْكُمْ أُمَّةٌ يَدْعُونَ إِلَى الْخَيْرِ وَيَأْمُرُونَ بِالْمَعْرُوفِ وَيَنْهَوْنَ عَنِ الْمُنْكَرِ}$$

"And let there arise amongst you a group, inviting to all that is good (Islam), enjoining al-Marouf (good) and forbidding (al-Munkar evil); and those are the ones whom are the successful". [Al- Imran: 104]

Allah's Messenger ﷺ said: **"The master of martyrs is Hamzah, and (equal to him) a man who stood up to an unjust ruler, commanded him (to do good) and forbade him (against evil) so (the ruler) killed him"**. And he said: **"There will be Ameer's, you recognise some of their actions (as Islamic) and you deny some. Whoever recognised (their munkar) he will be free from being associated to them, and whoever denied he will be safe of sin, but he who accepted (what they do) and followed (he will not be)"**. In another narration:

"Whoever **disliked (their munkar) he would be free (of responsibility), whoever denied he will be safe (of sin). But whoever accepted and followed, (he will not be").** The latter narration explains the first. These ahadith exclusively address struggle against the corrupt actions of the rulers. All of this is what is known as political struggle. These facts decisively command the engagement in political struggle. This is clear evidence that political struggle is an obligation.

Abandoning political struggle is a sin, for it is an abandonment of an obligation. There is no doubt that Allah 鐭 punishes for not performing it. There is also no doubt that whenever a people abandon it, they will be immersed in corruption and injustice. Establishing political struggle in life requires it's establishment in people. This is because when injustice dominates people for a long time and corruption increases among them, their tastes will be corrupted or they will become apathetic to it, and consequently they will no longer feel the pain of injustice or smell the stench of corruption. Also when the incentive of the Qur'an inside them weakens and they stay away from the Book of Allah 鐭 and the Sunnah of His Messenger, 鐭 the feeling of the gravity of the sin inside them dies. They will no longer feel their crime of abandoning what Allah 鐭 commanded. That is why urging people to engage in political struggle will bear no fruit's unless the fear of Allah 鐭 is revived in the hearts and feeling the pain of injustice and the gravity of sin is generated within them.

Political struggle is carried out by mouth and by anything that expresses discontent excluding fighting. Carrying out political struggle through fighting is forbidden except in the case where clear *Kufr* becomes apparent. In other words, when the Islamic lands ruled by Islam started to be ruled by *Kufr* or *Kufr* appears in the Islamic lands and the ruler remained silent. This means the clear *Kufr*, together with everything known among people as such when they have a decisive evidence from Allah 鐭 about it, where it appears while the lands are ruled by Islam. Other than this case, political struggle is to be done exclusively by mouth and whatever expresses discontent in order to create an opposing public opinion to *Kufr* in order to influence it, and consequently change it.

11
Political Actions

Struggle among states in times of peace, is done via political actions which may be accompanied by military action. Political actions that must be taken into consideration are those carried out by the superpowers. To this end there must exist information about the nature of the superpowers and important information about each of these powers.

The superpowers are those which have influence on international politics and perform actions that have an influence on other superpowers. Superpowers are not those which have a large population or those who are rich, rather the superpowers are those which influence international politics and other states. The political actions carried out by the states against each other in international struggle and international life are either to set international traps to weaken other states, or to carry out political manoeuvres, among others.

As a result, the politician must have a wide view that takes into consideration any action done by any superpower. When viewing political actions, the politician must keep away from absolutism and generalisation. The politician must relate every action to it's circumstances and all it's surrounding conditions. Hence, no action should be taken detached from it's surrounding conditions. Also, no issue should be comprehensively generalised or an action compared to another, nor should actions be placed in a logical sequence to reach logical conclusions. This must be avoided, for there is no bigger danger to political understanding than logic and comparison. This is because actions and life vary and each action has it's own circumstance and surrounding conditions. As a result, each action must be connected with the political information related to it and looked at within it's circumstances and surrounding conditions. This will ensure that it's understanding will be closer to the truth.

The political actions are those carried out to care for the affairs of the people, whether performed by individuals or parties and blocs, a state, or a group of states. Political actions have existed since groups emerged on earth. Tribes and leaders used to engage in political actions, and people will always be involved in performing political actions as long as there exist groups who care for their affairs. Therefore, engaging in political actions requires no particular political skill or mastership of the art of ruling. Rather, it is within the ability of every individual, group and state to perform political actions. However, the political actions that must be the centre of care and attention by any people who want to be liberated, or any *Ummah* who carries a message to mankind, are those related to the foreign countries, especially those actions related to struggle against the colonialist nations and for protecting itself against the states with ill intentions. Consequently, it is mandatory that the Islamic *Ummah*, while working to liberate herself and to carry the Islamic Da'wah, pays great attention to the actions related to the foreign powers. It should place these actions ahead of all other actions and at the top of all priorities.

Reviewing the political actions in the past and the present, we find that they filled history. As a matter of fact, history in it's entirety is but a series of political actions. It is the political actions that presently busy the world. It is these that guarantee victory to states and elevate the status of peoples and nations. Often they eliminated the need for armies in conquests. So when the Messenger ﷺ offered himself to the tribes, took the second pledge of allegiance, sent Abdullah ibn Jahsh to find out the news of Makkah, and went to take the caravan of Quraysh which led to the battle of Badr, he was only undertaking political actions. Also when he ﷺ sent Naeem to discourage the tribes and spread doubt amongst them in the battle of Khandaq (the trench), went for Umrah and stayed in Hudaybiyah, when he appointed Saad bin Muath a judge over Bani Quraythah, he was only performing political actions. When Al-Abbass brought Abu Sufyan on his way to Makkah, he signed the treaties, received envoys from the Arabian peninsula, did *Mubahalah* (contesting with another and cursing the liar) with the Christians who visited him, ordered the expulsion and evacuation of Banu Nadheer from their homes and re-appointed the ruler of Yemen after he became a Muslim.

All of these are but political actions. The same applies to the rightly guided Khulafaa and the Khulafaa after them. What dominated their actions with the foreign nations were political actions. It is due to this fact, that when Allah's Messenger, 霺 used to appoint an Ameer of an army, he would command him to demand from the people to embrace Islam. If they refused, he offered them to pay *Jizzyah*. If they still rejected the offer he would perform prayer of *Istikharah* and warn them of war. So, this was the last action resorted to.

Political actions should always be performed first. Hence, political actions are of the most important duties of the *Ummah* and are of utmost priority. Consequently, it should not be seen strange that political actions are the most important actions for liberation and the carrying of the Islamic Da'wah. Had it not been for political actions, Islam would not have spread nor would it be possible to carry it to mankind today.

Performing political actions today requires that the *Ummah* be aware of the relations among nations. She should keep up with these relations, and comprehend their secrets and objectives. She should differentiate between what is a manoeuvre, and what is not a manoeuvre and distinguish an action from it's goals. She should be aware of the latest form of relations. This requires the continuous political culturing of the *Ummah*, making her keep up and comprehend the foreign politics constantly and realistically. It also requires that carrying the Islamic Da'wah is the final criterion that determines and runs this policy.

12

Political Experience

In order for a person to be a politician, he must have political experience. This is irrespective whether he were to involve himself in politics and conducts it as a politician who deserves this title, or he does not engage in politics, like the academic politician. For a person to acquire political experience, he must possess three important matters: 1) Political information, 2) continuous knowledge of the current political news, 3) a good choice of political news.

As for the political information, it refers to historical information, especially historical facts, information about events, and actions and individuals related to these matters from the political perspective. Also information about political relations amongst individuals or states, and thoughts must be known. This information reveals the meaning of the political thought be it news, action or a principle; and whether this principle is a creed or a rule. Without such information the political thought cannot be understood regardless of the intelligence or ingenuity of the person. This is so, because the issue is a matter of understanding, and not intelligence.

With regard to the need for current news, especially the political news, this is so because they are information and news about current events, and they are the subject for understanding and study, that must be known. Since life's affairs vary, change, differ and contradict, they must be followed in order to maintain awareness of them. In other words they must be known so that the politician is aware of them, i.e. so that he stands at the train station that the train would be passing through at that moment. Without this updated knowledge he would be standing at a station that the train had passed through an hour ago, and was now passing another station. Therefore, it is necessary to follow up (pursue) the news continuously where no single item is missed, whether important or trivial. He must go through the pain of looking for a needle in a haystack which he may not find. One does not know when important news will occur. So he must follow up all the news, important or unimportant, to him, for they are rings of a chain that are connected together, where if a ring is lost, the chain would be broken and then it would be difficult to understand the subject. If the chain is broken, he might wrongly understand the subject and thus connect the situation to news or a thought that had expired and no longer exists. Because of this one must pursue the news in a continuous fashion, to be able to understand politics. As for the proper selection of news, it is achieved when the politician considers it. The politician does not consider all news he receives. He only considers the important news, for he has to distinguish between the news to consider, and that to disregard, even though he listens to all news. He will only consider the useful news. Useless news must not be considered even if it forms information. This is the point of following the news for the purpose of considering it, not just for listening to it.

13

Involvement in Politics is an Obligation Upon Muslims

Allah's Messenger ﷺ said: "**There will be leaders**", "**No as long as they pray**", and: "**The best type of Jihad is a word of Haqq said to an unjust ruler or leader**". He also said: "**The leader of martyrs is Hamza ibn Abdul Muttalib. Equivalent to him is a man that stood up to an unjust ruler, commanded him (to do good) and forbade him (from doing evil) and he (the ruler) killed him**". Also, Ubadah ibn As-Samit said: The Prophet called upon us and we gave him the *Bay'ah*. Part of the pledge he took from us was to hear and obey in our active time and non- active time, in hardship or ease....

Allah ﷻ said:

الم * غُلِبَتْ الرُّومُ * فِي أَدْنَى
الأَرْضِ وَهُمْ مِنْ بَعْدِ غَلَبِهِمْ
سَيَغْلِبُونَ * فِي بِضْعِ سِنِينَ لِلَّهِ
الأَمْرُ مِنْ قَبْلُ وَمِنْ بَعْدُ وَيَوْمَئِذٍ
يَفْرَحُ الْمُؤْمِنُونَ *

"Alif - Lam - Mim.
The Romans have been defeated. In the nearer land, and they, after their defeat, will be victorious. Within three to nine years. The decision of the matter, before and after is only with Allah. And on that Day, the believers will rejoice". [Ar- Rum: 1 - 4]

The above Ahadith and honourable ayah are the evidences that involvement in politics is an obligation upon Muslims. This is because Siyasah linguistically is caring for peoples affairs. Caring for Muslims only means caring for their affairs. Caring for their affairs means to look after them and to know what the ruler governs the people by. Objecting to the rulers actions is indulging in politics and is caring for Muslims' affairs. Commanding the unjust ruler to do good, and forbidding him from doing evil, is caring for Muslims' affairs and looking after their affairs. Also opposing the one in charge is not but caring for, and looking after Muslims affairs.

The command in these Ahadith is decisive. This means that Allah 🕮 decisively commanded the believers to care for Muslims i.e. to engage in politics.

Involvement in politics is for protecting the Muslims against the harm caused by the ruler and by the enemy. It is due to this that the Ahadith are not confined to protecting the Muslims from the harm of the ruler but also the harm of the enemies. Jareer ibn Abdullah said: I came to the Prophet and said: I give you the *Bayah* to Islam. He 🕮 stipulated for me to give advice (*Nush*) to every Muslim. The word *Nush* in the hadith is inclusive and thus includes giving the Muslim the advice by protecting him against the rulers harm as well as the enemies harm.

This means that Muslims must engage in the internal politics i.e. being aware of the way the rulers care for the peoples affairs in order to account them. This also means that Muslims are to engage in foreign politics by being aware of what the disbelieving countries plot against Muslims in order to expose their plan and act to protect the *Ummah* and stop all harm. Therefore, the obligation of engaging in politics is not restricted to internal politics but includes external politics as well. So the obligation is to engage in politics be it internal or external. Moreover, the verses: *Alif - Lam - Mim.*
The Romans have been defeated. In the nearer land, and they, after their defeat, will be victorious [Ar- Rum: 1 - 3] clearly indicate the extent of attention the Messenger 🕮 and the honourable Sahabah gave to foreign politics and international affairs. Ibn Abi Hatim reported from Ibn Shibab that he said: We were informed that the Mushrikeen used to argue with the Muslims in Makkah before the Messenger left for Medina. They used to say: The Romans believe they are a people of a Book and the Majus (magi) defeated the Romans who are a people of a Book, we will defeat you in the same way. Then Allah 🕮 revealed: *"Alif lam meem, The Romans were defeated.."*. This proves that Muslims in Makkah before the establishment of the Islamic state, used to argue with the non-believers

regarding the news of other states and international relations. It was reported that Abu Bakr had placed a bet with the Mushriks that the Romans would be victorious. He informed the Messenger ﷺ of his bet. The Messenger approved his action, asked him to extend the time and he placed himself as a partner in the bet. This shows that knowing the affairs of the states of the time and the relations among them was performed by the Muslims and approved by the Messenger ﷺ.

In addition, to that, the *Ummah* must carry the Islamic Da'wah to the world. The *Ummah* will not be able to carry it's call to the world unless she is aware of the policies of the other states. Therefore, general knowledge of world politics and the policies of every state that the *Ummah* either wants to carry the Da'wah to, or protect herself against, is an obligation of *Kifayah* (sufficiency) upon Muslims. This is due to the fact that carrying the Da'wah is an obligation, as is protecting the *Ummah* against the enemies plots. This cannot be achieved except by understanding world politics and the policies of the states with which we are concerned, in order to carry the Da'wah to their population or to stop their plots. The divine rule states: the requirement to fulfil an obligation is itself an obligation. Therefore, engaging in international politics is an obligation of *Kifayah* upon Muslims.

Since the *Ummah* is legally obliged to carry the Islamic Da'wah to all peoples, it is mandatory upon Muslims to remain in contact with the world while being aware of it's situation, realising it's problems, knowledgeable of the motives of it's countries and peoples, pursuing current political actions, observing the political plans of the states regarding their styles of execution and their relationships with each other, and the political manoeuvres carried out by these states.

In addition, the rulers' actions with the other countries are part of the foreign policy. Thus, they are included in accounting the ruler re: his actions with the other states. The rule 'that which is required to achieve an obligation, is itself an obligation' shows that being aware of the states' activities and their actions to care for the *Ummah*'s affairs in ruling and foreign policy is an obligation. This is because it is not possible to engage in internal and external politics i.e. accounting the rulers for their internal and external actions except by being aware of their actions. If their actions are not truly known, it is not possible to engage in politics.

Based on all of the above, it becomes clear that engaging in politics, whether internal or external, is an obligation of *Kifayah* upon Muslims. If this obligation is not performed, they would be sinful.

14
The Statesman

Most people think that the statesman is the ruler or the person engaged in ruling in the state. As a result, they gave this description to the head of the state, ministers and their like. They do not consider others as statesmen. Also, they categorise the people into two types: the statesman and the ordinary person and they include all officials and employees of the state in the second category.

This understanding of the statesman held by the people is erroneous. The ruler might be a statesman or may not. The ordinary person could be a statesman even if he does not engage in any of the ruling functions. He may be a farmer on his farm, a worker in a factory, a merchant, or a teacher and yet still be a statesman.

The statesman is the creative political leader. He is the person who possesses the ruling mentality and is able to manage the state's affairs, solve problems and control the private and public relations. This is the statesman. He could be present amongst the people and not be a ruler, nor performing any ruling functions.

The Islamic state, since it's establishment in the first year of *Hijrah*, was rich with a large number of men who held this description in their mentalities, disposition and behaviour. This continued for over six centuries i.e. towards the end of the Abbassid state. Even after that point in time, individuals with a statesman like mentality continued to exist until the middle of the eleventh century (18 CE) when the deficiency in developing the statesmen like mentality started. The number of men who could truly be called statesman became few. Upon the collapse of the Khilafah, the number was not only few, but even the soil that would produce such statesman ceased to exist. The *Ummah* no longer produced men with statesman like mentalities and therefore they no longer existed in the *Ummah*.

The *Ummah* in which the statesman develops is that which enjoys the ideas of ruling in her practical life's affairs, as well as internal and external relations, and has the sense of responsibility for all peoples. Her responsibility extends to those outside of her borders. For looking after their affairs and solving their problems she must have a sense of her own value among nations, as a result of which, she rushes to be in the leading position in the whole world.

This is the soil in which the statesman and the ruling mentality grows. It is summarised in three points:

(a) She must practically have in her life a specific point of view that forms a comprehensive idea.
(b) She must practically have a specific point of view in life which guarantees happiness in reality.
(c) She must have a particular culture (*Hadarah*) that uplifts the people to live in the most elevated situation, best form of living, and the highest aspects of thought coupled with the high values and permanent tranquillity.

The above three points are definitely available to Muslims in the form of books and the minds of the scholars. They need to be transferred to the practical aspect of life. The one who transfers them to reality is the statesman. This is due to the fact that the statesman is the creative political leader, and because the political thought must have a political leadership to exist in life. The presence of political thought in books and the minds of scholars would be of no value and would not be an actual presence. For a political leadership to exist, there must exist someone who understands the political thought creatively, engages in using it without hypocrisy, with creativity one of his innate merit's.

It is true that this *Ummah* still possesses a comprehensive thought about man, life and the universe. It is the greatest comprehensive idea, i.e. the greatest Aqeedah. It is also true that she has a specific point of view in life that guarantees happiness for the Muslim. The Islamic *Ummah* has a unique culture (*Hadarah*) that uplifts the Muslims to live in the highest standards of life, and the highest levels of thought. Though the *Ummah* possesses all of the above, it is not put into practice or applied. They have turned to mere philosophical ideas present in books and information kept in the minds of scholars.

As a result, the soil that produces statesmen no longer exists. So it is only natural for such people to be scarce. For how could the Muslim have political leadership if he is not fed with the concepts of leadership or political thoughts? How could he be creative, while he runs breathlessly seeking his own benefit rather than taking care (of peoples' affairs), and seeking the approval of the superpowers rather than competing with and challenging them.

In order for Muslims to achieve revival, they must look for the way to develop statesmen, and increase their numbers. This cannot be achieved unless they culture themselves with the political culture that is based on the Islamic Aqeedah, i.e. based on the comprehensive idea about man, life and the universe. Once this culture prevails amongst the Muslim masses, and has a reality, then the soil that produces statesmen, will exist. Only then will the rich growth of the statesmen begin. Once these men exist, revival exists and change exists or almost exists.

This is the statesman, and this is the situation or atmosphere in which he develops. The statesman is not necessarily the ruler. Rather, he is the creative political leader who grows in the *Ummah*. He is not the one who is appointed through elections or a military coup or through his wealth, yet is not aware of his surroundings and does not see beyond his nose.

As for how the statesman gets to power, he must impose himself on those around him first and then upon his country or province. Then he might be appointed to rule after his ability and suitability becomes known. He may also gain power through elections, though this only exists in the sincere states with aware people. However, in such countries as those of the current Islamic world, the way for the statesman to reach power is that he should work first to take the leadership of the people, establish out of them a group of influential people through which he can threaten the existing government, and finally overthrow it and take charge. As for the elections that currently take place in our countries, they only bring people who are comparable to the existing rulers in their shallowness and absurdity.

When Muslims used to implement Islam and culture themselves with it, they produced thousands of people who were qualified to be statesmen. Some of them were in a position of ruling, such as Umar, Ali, Al-Mu'tasim, Salah ud-Deen, and Muhammad al -Fatih. Others remained as ordinary citizens without an official job such as, Ibn Abbas, Al-Ahhaf ibn Qays, Ahmad ibn Hanbal and Ibn Taymiyyah. All of them proceeded from the Aqeedah of Islam, followed the political path, enjoined the sense of responsibility towards all mankind in terms of guiding them and delivering the Islamic call to all of them, implementing Islam upon them, in addition to their responsibility for the internal affairs of the *Ummah*. There is the saying of Umar ibn Al-Khattab, (ra) 'If an animal, in the land of Iraq, trips, I would be afraid that Allah ﷻ would account me, for not fixing the road for it'. Al-Mu'tasim heard of a Muslim woman in the Roman land screaming his name, and he rushed to her rescue. He personally headed an army conquering the Roman lands till he conquered the birth place of their emperor. And there is Ahmad ibn Hanbal who was severely beaten and harassed in order to force him to adopt the opinion of the creation of the Qur'an. He preferred to be beaten and imprisoned rather than say such a thing that would let the Muslims go astray. Such feeling of responsibility is a required condition for the statesman.

Today, however, Muslims are plagued with many illnesses, the least of which is not the absence of the statesman. In the absence of the statesman nowadays, other rulers and people of power have appeared. None of them can be described as a statesman in any fashion. They are unable to think and plan, and carry out the interests of the *Ummah*. They leave all of that to the superpowers to do on their behalf, and enable them to use their country's resources. These rulers have almost become like employees and hired hands. Under these circumstances, these superpowers started spreading their capitalist, communist, patriotic and nationalistic ideas, and made expediency dominate their relations. As a result, matters became confused, and originality in thinking and ruling disappeared, and imitation, which is the path of the weak and incapable, became dominant. This verified the saying of the honourable Prophet ﷺ, **"You will follow the ways of those before you hand span by hand span and yard by yard, even if they entered a lizards hole you would enter it, and even if they slept with their wives in the road, you would do it"**. The rulers as well as many people no longer base their thinking, behaviour and solutions on the Islamic Aqeedah. They have embarked on the Western ideas and read the ideas of ruling from the dominating countries. They took the Book of The Prince as their covenant and Machiavelli as their guide. They started repeating what they read without understanding that these ideas were suitable in a capitalist or communist society but not suitable for the Islamic *Ummah*. They fit the saying of Messenger of Allah ﷺ, "**Deceiving years will come where the people would believe the liar and not believe the trustworthy, and the traitor would be trusted and the honest would be distrusted. In those years, the *Ruwaybidah* will speak**". He was asked, "And what is *Ruwaybidah*? He ﷺ said, "**The shallow man who speaks about the public affairs**".

15
Political Medium

The political medium is that which exists among those who keep up with the political news, political activities and events so as to give their views regarding them and care for the peoples affairs according to these views. In other words, this is the medium of politicians, whether rulers or not. The medium in which they live and act is what is referred to as the political medium.

The political medium varies with the difference in ideas by which people are ruled and by which their affairs are cared for. It also varies according to the difference in the level of civilisation. So, the countries that are ruled by capitalist ideas have a political medium different from that of the country which is ruled by communist ideas, and different from that of the countries which are ruled by Islamic ideas. Also, the countries that have a flourishing civilisation will have a political medium that is different from that present in the country where civilisation is weak or lagging. Thus, the political medium in a country like France is different from that in a country like Russia, and the political medium in a country like Abyssinia is different from that in a country like Canada. However, the political medium in a country such as the United States is similar to that in a country like Lebanon, even though these countries vary in the degree of liberation and independence. As stated above, the political medium is that of those who keep up with the news and judge it in accordance with the points of view and ideas they have about peoples affairs and how to care for them. The politicians in a country like the U.S. carry the ideas of freedom and capitalism. Their goal is the individual achievement in life. Therefore, they are fully liberal. They consider accounting the ruler as an inseparable part of their political life and the aggressive criticism of their rulers and others as one of their rights. This differs from the politicians in a country like Russia in the days of Communism and the Soviet Union, where they carry the ideas of collective achievement, not individualism and the idea of communism.

Their primary concern is the protection of their group. They view others as enemies and opponents. As a result, one finds in the political medium of America opposition and plots against the rulers there, as well as against other countries even if they were capitalist like them.

This medium is different from the political medium in Russia, where there is no opposition. Political criticism of their rulers or of other states is not allowed. Therefore, the political medium in the U.S. is not restricted to the rulers and those who care for the peoples affairs. Rather, it is inclusive of the rulers and others. It includes also those who care for the peoples affairs in practice or care for their affairs in speech and thought.

Therefore, the political medium addressed here is that which can be lived in and is amongst it's people. It is not that which is exclusive to the rulers. In other words, it is the open political medium which any person can enter. It is not the closed political medium that is not open to the public.

There is no Islamic political medium today due to the absence of countries that are ruled by the Islamic thoughts. A quick look at the Islamic history, especially in the first era, shows that there used to exist an Islamic medium when Muslims used to rule by Islamic thoughts. This was especially the case when Islam was understood as it was by the successors of the Prophet ﷺ in their first era, when they succeeded the Messenger ﷺ in reality and were *Khulafaa* and not merely rulers.

Since the Islamic state will certainly be re-established and it is merely a matter of time, it is mandatory upon those who work to establish the rule of Islam to first envisage the Islamic political medium. Also, they must work to establish such a medium so that they do not go astray from the Islamic political medium as they did from the ruling system of Islam.

A quick look at the thoughts of Islam, part of which are the thoughts related to the ruling system, reflects that they are political thoughts. This is especially true since they were established in life as political thoughts. Even thoughts which are related to the Aqeedah are political thoughts. Therefore, the entire Islamic political medium is almost a political medium. Furthermore, in the country that is ruled by Islam, an Islamic political medium will naturally and inevitably exist. This is true historically as well as in the reality that must be lived in by Muslims. Therefore, envisaging the Islamic political medium that existed in the past is possible by studying the events of political mediums. It is also possible presently by studying the Islamic thoughts. As for working to create this medium, especially once the Islamic state is established, it requires attention and requires engaging in and practising political awareness and exercising it in life.

The first step in working to create the Islamic political medium is to have people who keep up with the political news, actions and events in the world. They should keep up with the news to comprehend it and then try to care for the people's affairs according to it, whilst being committed to the meaning of this caring from the viewpoint of Islam. Once such people with these qualities exist, then the first step in creating this medium and what is related to it has taken place. Whilst the state will definitely lead to it's existence and it's presence or creation is required for the state, the basic issue is to have pursuance of political news and this should be used to foster peoples affairs according to the thoughts of Islam.

Needless to say, that the goal of following up the news and analysing it is to give the people an opinion regarding it. Whoever does not keep up with news can not be a politician. Consequently, such a person cannot work to create a political medium, for one cannot give something if he does not have it.

The one who pursues the news without analysing it is like the one who pursues the news merely for the purpose of knowledge; this person harms himself and his *Ummah*, for when he gives his opinions according to how the news appears and without analysis, he becomes misled and misleads others. Therefore, analysing the news is necessary to keeping up with it. However, limiting oneself to pursuing the news, analysing it, and then reporting it to the people does not make the person a politician. Such a person would not be able to work to create the political medium nor function in it, and merely makes him a news reporter and analyst, i.e. a source of news and good understanding of it but not a politician. Therefore, one must link pursuance and analysis of the news with giving ones opinion regarding the news to the people. Consequently, it becomes clear that the goal of following and analysing the news is to give an opinion regarding it to the people. This is self evident or must be so.

Giving an opinion regarding news should not be from a neutral point of view or a mere presentation of an understanding. Rather, it must be based on a particular point of view about life. In other words, it must emanate from or be based on political awareness. Only then will the given opinion be a political one that has weight and value. Giving one's opinion in this fashion is what makes it caring for the peoples affairs.

Therefore, for any person to be a politician and be able to work to create or function in a political medium, four conditions must be fulfilled;

(a) Political news
(b) Analysis of the news
(c) Give his opinion regarding it to the people
(d) Have this opinion result from or be based on a particular viewpoint of life.

Unless all of these four points are present, the Islamic political medium will not exist nor is it possible to function in any political medium. Whilst following up the political news is the first step, political awareness or giving an opinion from a particular angle related to the viewpoint of life, is what makes the first step exist completely.

Needless to say, the disbelieving states have not only eliminated the Islamic political medium but also filled the Muslims with aversion to politics itself and distanced them away from following up the news. This is clear to everyone. Also, it is needless to say that the current political medium closes it's gates to anyone who gives the political opinion based on the Islamic point of view of life; and then it is not opened for him willingly. Even though this might not be noticed by the people in a tangible way, those who pursue the news and try to give the Islamic opinion, witness how the gates of the political medium are shut in their faces, even in the countries that claim they call for freedom. Accordingly the issue is not merely following up and analysing or even giving the opinion from a certain angle, but rather is to enter into the political medium in the Islamic countries even against the will of those who close it's gates, and even if it costs dearly to enter.

An issue that must be made the subject of discussion and attention is the creation of the Islamic political medium in the Islamic countries. The Islamic political medium will definitely come into existence once the Islamic state is established. However, entering the political mediums before the establishment of the state or the annexation of an Islamic country to it, is mandated by working to establish Islam in life and specifically in the political medium. Consequently, working to enter the political medium in any Islamic country is fundamental for anyone who works politically for Islam.

Political mediums in non-Islamic countries are corrupt. The least to say about them is that they function in accordance with the slogan, the ends justify the means, and that they are Machiavellian in nature and method. In addition, selfishness and personal interests are manifest in their men. Therefore, there is nothing good in them that tempts us to imitate them. Moreover, we carry a message to save their countries and peoples. As for the political mediums in the Islamic countries, not only do they have the corruption of the Western political mediums, but also they contain agents and imitators fascinated with the *Kufr* systems and policies, who are filled with hatred, grudges and contempt for Islam. Therefore, it is not sufficient to attempt to enter this medium but we must work to destroy it and convert it to an Islamic medium. It is true that it is possible to work for this from outside these mediums, but working for this from within is easier and more productive. However, even though the men of the political mediums in the Islamic countries are of no significance in comparison with the men of the West and the Western political mediums, they are considered great in the Islamic countries. As a matter of fact, they are giants in the eyes of their people, because they are the rulers or the leaders or those who have great influence on the life of the people and their living. Also, they have enough intelligence, knowledge and expertise to put them ahead of the people, and sufficient shrewdness and improvisation to adapt themselves to any situation. Thus they pray in the first line in the masjid the five daily prayers if Islam is what dominates the society. So, it is possible that in the Islamic state, such people may become the first who work for it and become leaders of the Islamic movement. It is clear that these people have no sincerity and are skilled in hiding their hypocrisy. Also, they are most capable in causing destruction and the most experienced in leading countries and sincere politicians to collapse. Once the Islamic state is established, if these politicians still exist, they might show the *Ummah* sincerity and understanding that would make them leaders in the political mediums. Therefore, their influence must be terminated to shield ourselves from their threat.

In the recent history, we have seen that when America attempted to remove the British from some of the Islamic lands, it attempted to eliminate the old political medium. It struck against the old political medium in Egypt and Iraq by assassination, imprisonment and threatening their livelihood. It was, to a certain degree, able to dilute their threat and limit their harm, but was unable to eliminate them completely. Thus, the old political medium continued to exist in Egypt and Iraq, even though hidden like fire under the ashes. This was due to the fact that America and it's agents did not create a political medium to replace the old one. Regardless of the attempts to eliminate the political medium and prevent it from surfacing, the regime can not wipe it out. This is because the political medium is the twin of every rule like a shadow to man. Therefore, wherever there exists authority, a political medium will exist.

Upon the arrival of the Messenger of Allah ﷺ in Medinah, the political medium was created by embracing Islam and readiness to support it. The old political medium collapsed, that of Abdullah ibn Ubai and his likes. When the Messenger ﷺ conquered Makkah, he eliminated the then existing political medium by war, and stripped those who survived from any influence. Muslims replaced them and became the leaders and consequently the new political medium was created and the old one was eliminated.

The Islamic state must remove all political mediums by any means necessary, such as striking peoples necks or threatening their livelihood or eliminating their political and moral entities, among other means. This is mandated by the laws of the universe and required by establishing Dar-ul-Islam and terminating Dar-ul-*Kufr*. This, however, is not sufficient until political Islamic mediums exist, composed of the aware and sincere Muslims, and not the hypocrites. If the aware and sincere Muslims limited themselves to keeping up with, and analysing the news, they can not form a political medium with that alone. Those who were in the political mediums in Dar-ul-*Kufr* and managed to survive, will be more capable to lead the new political mediums, let alone creating them and entering them. Then, the seed of the destruction of the state would be sown as soon as the state is created.

Not only are the aware and sincere Muslims prevented from entering the political medium, even in the Islamic state, but also the hypocrites would be encouraged to create and lead the political mediums. Therefore, if the sincere and aware Muslims do not go beyond following up the news and analysing it and giving their opinion from a particular angle and then attempting to enter the political mediums, it is feared that they would stay outside the house, even though it is theirs, which they created and is exclusive to them.

The issue today, for the sincere and aware Muslims, is no longer becoming politicians. The issue for them now is to attempt to create the Islamic political medium. Regardless of how long it takes, the Islamic state will definitely be established. It is feared that once the Islamic state is established, people of the current political medium and the insincere politicians may precede them in creating the Islamic political medium, which must be created and composed of them alone. Also, prior to the establishment of the Islamic state, the sincere and aware Muslims live on the margins of society and the people. Unless they are able to establish Islamic political mediums or enter the current political mediums for the purpose of changing them, they will continue to be on the margins, and they will have no presence, effective or other. Therefore, the present, with all it's pain and deprivation, and the future with all that it carries of hope and glory, mandate that the aware and sincere people realise the importance of being politicians, especially that their party forces itself upon the people as a political party, and not merely as an aware movement. It is true that the Messenger ﷺ did not create the political medium except in Medinah, after the establishment of the state. And it is true that the savage persecution against the *Shabab* of the *Hizb* by the rulers in every Islamic land does not enable the sincere and aware people from moving politically. It is also true that the bulk of the aware and sincere people are not from the influential or educated class, or from the aged and experienced. But the Sahabah in Makkah still attempted to enter into the political medium. The discussion between Abu Bakr (ra) and the leaders of Quraysh about the issue of the Persians and the Romans was an attempt to enter the political medium. And the statement

Umar made to the people of Makkah, "Once we become 300 persons either we throw you out of it (Makkah) or you throw us out", was also an example of the struggle to look after the affairs of the people. The savage persecution and harm inflicted by Quraysh upon the Muslims needs no elaboration. As for whether they were from the high class in Makkah or not, Abu Bakr (ra) used to carry old clothes on his shoulders in the markets to sell them. None of them were from the influential people except Hamza (ra) and Umar (ra). Yet, once they became Muslims they lost that status. As for the sincere Sahaba being young in age, youth does not prevent people from being intelligent.

Therefore, there is no excuse for the sincere and aware people not to work to be politicians, and attempting to enter the political medium. Time runs fast and must be beaten. The enemies and opponents of Islam are the enemies and opponents of the sincere and aware in the first instance. The aware and sincere must be as strong in their ideas as they are in their Aqeedah, and as daring in their attitude as they are in their understanding and comprehension. Otherwise, victory might come to other than them, even though they paved the way for victory; and they may remain away from the true battlefield of life.

Consequently, following up the news, analysing it, giving an opinion regarding it, and making sure that such an opinion is always given from a specific angle, this would ensure that it is the aware and sincere who represent the moment, future, and the awaited hope for the people.

16
Vacuum

The word vacuum is a term used in international politics. It means the inability to function or to stay stable. So, while there is a power, it does not manifest the proper appearance or suitable ability. There are various types of vacuum: political, military, and strategic.

Political vacuum refers to the state in it's entirety is unstable and incohesive. While there might exist a head of state, prime minister or representatives of the *Ummah*, there is no harmony among them due to the lack of coherence between their ideas and actions. This results in an incohesive state where the actions of the people in power lack harmony. Also, there may be no stable opinion, action or attitude towards challenges. This will result in a vacuum, meaning it is as if the state does not exist. In this case, looking for another state, (i.e. rulers) is something natural and maybe inevitable. Another power will come forward to fill the vacuum. This power might be independent, domestic, or external; or it may be domestic but holds power with the help of a foreign support which it relies on.

As for the military vacuum, it occurs in the case where the states military power is not sufficient to keep the internal security and protect the state against an external attack. So it cannot defend itself against internal rebellion or external invasion. The states inability to defend itself or maintain it's stability arises from one or both of two reasons:

(1) Insufficient military equipment, training or wealth which would enable the state to prepare the necessary military power. This will result in a military vacuum i.e. as if the military power is non-existent. In this case, fear of the domination of foreign powers over the country would be expected. Usually, such powers would have ambitions in this country and the strongest amongst them would rush to occupy it. To prevent such an occupation from taking place,

another competing power would rush to arm the country suffering from the military vacuum. If the vacuum is not filled by this means, the occupation will take place and the vacuum will be filled by a completely foreign power.

(2) Lack of harmony amongst the army personnel or it's leadership, and the inability to function or to remain stable. In such a case, a foreign power would come in and support one army member or faction morally and strategically. This would fill the vacuum by the foreign power indirectly. If the vacuum is not filled in this way, it will be filled directly by a foreign power, as in the first case. Therefore,a military vacuum occurs when the existing military power in a country has demonstrated it's inability to function, or to remain stable. This is either due to the lack of harmony and stability amongst the army's commanders and officers, or due to the inadequacy of material force necessary for defence and security.

As for the strategic vacuum it is the instability of a country resulting from problems and challenges faced in terms of internal and external security. For example, there might exist in the country conflicting wings that clash with each other physically and they might even use arms. Or activities that threaten the security may occur, such as planting bombs in a continuous fashion in different areas. Or it might occur through the spread of rumours that instigate worry among the businessmen, traders, and amongst the politicians and rulers, or amongst the people particularly for their foodstuffs. Sometimes, instability is created by sporadic foreign aggression that is not aimed at occupation of the country but at keeping it troubled and preoccupied. Such situations would result in a vacuum i.e. as if the state does not exist. In this case, it becomes natural to look for a state that would guarantee stability, so a power would attempt to fill this vacuum. This power could be individuals from inside who would come to power and secure stability independently, or from a foreign state which would take over the country and secure stability. Or it may be individuals from within the state whom are brought to power and supported by a foreign state who establish stability and fill the vacuum.

The vacuum by the above three meanings is a powerful weapon which is extremely effective. The superpowers attempt to create instability in every country they try to subjugate and control. The Ottoman state was specifically exhausted by the attempts to create a vacuum, not by the war.

17
Ruling in Islam

Ruling (*Al-Hukm*) linguistically means judging (*Al-Gada'a*). The ruler (*Haakim*) is the one who executes the rule (*Hukm*). Conventionally, *Hukm, Mulk* and *Sultan* have the same meaning which is the authority that implements the rules. In other words, it is the task of leadership (*Imaarah*) which the Shari'ah obliged Muslims to have. This *Imaarah's* job is the authority used to prevent injustice and settle disputes. In other words, *Hukm* is the *Wilayat-al-amr* mentioned in the saying of Allah, ﷻ *"Obey Allah, and obey the Messenger and Ulil-al-amr from among you"* It is also mentioned in His saying, *"had they referred it to the Messenger and Ulil-al-amr from among them"*. Ruling therefore, is the actual caring for the affairs.

Islam, being an ideology for the state, society, and life, made ruling and the state an integral part of it. It commanded Muslims to establish the state and to rule by the laws of Islam. Tens of ayat of al-Qur'an al-Kareem were revealed pertaining to ruling and authority, commanding Muslims to rule by that which Allah ﷻ has revealed.

Allah ﷻ says,

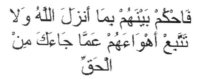

"And rule among them by what Allah has revealed and follow not their desires away from the Truth which has come to you". [Al- Maidah: 48]

وَأَنْ احْكُمْ بَيْنَهُمْ بِمَا أَنزَلَ اللَّهُ
وَلَا تَتَّبِعْ أَهْوَاءَهُمْ وَاحْذَرْهُمْ أَنْ
يَفْتِنُوكَ عَنْ بَعْضِ مَا أَنزَلَ اللَّهُ
إِلَيْكَ

"And rule among them by what Allah has revealed and follow not their desires and beware that they might seduce you from some of what Allah has revealed to you". [Al- Maidah: 49]

وَمَنْ لَمْ يَحْكُمْ بِمَا أَنزَلَ اللَّهُ
فَأُوْلَئِكَ هُمُ الْكَافِرُونَ

"And whoever does not rule by that which Allah has revealed, they are Kafirs". [Al- Maidah: 44]

He ﷺ also said,

وَمَنْ لَمْ يَحْكُمْ بِمَا أَنزَلَ اللَّهُ
فَأُوْلَئِكَ هُمُ الظَّالِمُونَ

"And whoever does not rule by that which Allah has revealed, they are Thalims". [Al- Maidah: 45]

and

وَمَنْ لَمْ يَحْكُمْ بِمَا أنزلَ اللَّهُ
فَأُوْلَئِكَ هُمُ الْفَاسِقُونَ

"And whoever does not rule by that which Allah has revealed, they are Fasiqs". [Al- Maidah: 47]

And He 🕮 said,

$$فَلَا وَرَبِّكَ لَا يُؤْمِنُونَ حَتَّى$$
$$يُحَكِّمُوكَ فِيمَا شَجَرَ بَيْنَهُمْ ثُمَّ لَا$$
$$يَجِدُوا فِي أَنْفُسِهِمْ حَرَجًا مِمَّا$$
$$قَضَيْتَ وَيُسَلِّمُوا تَسْلِيمًا$$

"But no by your Lord, they can have no Faith, until they make you (Oh Muhammad), judge in all disputes between them, and find in themselves no resistance against your decisions, and accept (them) with full submission". [An- Nisa: 65]

$$يَاأَيُّهَا الَّذِينَ آمَنُوا أَطِيعُوا اللَّهَ$$
$$وَأَطِيعُوا الرَّسُولَ وَأُولِي الْأَمْرِ$$
$$مِنْكُمْ$$

"Oh you who believe! Obey Allah and the Messenger, and those of you who are in authority. And if you differ in anything amongst yourselves, refer it to Allah and His Messenger, if you believe in Allah and in the Last Day. That is better and more suitable for final determination". [An- Nisa: 59]

and,

$$وَإِذَا حَكَمْتُمْ بَيْنَ النَّاسِ أَنْ$$
$$تَحْكُمُوا بِالْعَدْلِ$$

"If you (Muslims) judge among people, you should judge with justice".
[An- Nisa: 58]

In addition to the above, there are tens of ayat related to ruling and authority. Also, there are many ayat which indicate details concerning the incidents of ruling. Thus there are verses regarding military, political, criminal, social and civil legislation.

Allah ﷻ says:

يَاأَيُّهَا الَّذِينَ آمَنُوا قَاتِلُوا الَّذِينَ
يَلُونَكُمْ مِنْ الْكُفَّارِ وَلْيَجِدُوا فِيكُمْ
غِلْظَةً

"Oh you who believe, fight those who are near to you of the disbelievers, and let them find harshness in you". [At- Tauba: 123]

He ﷻ said:

فَإِمَّا تَثْقَفَنَّهُمْ فِي الْحَرْبِ فَشَرِّدْ
بِهِمْ مَنْ خَلْفَهُمْ لَعَلَّهُمْ يَذَّكَّرُونَ *
وَإِمَّا تَخَافَنَّ مِنْ قَوْمٍ خِيَانَةً فَانْبِذْ
إِلَيْهِمْ عَلَى سَوَاءٍ

"If you gain mastery over them in war, disperse with them those who follow them, that they may remember. If you fear treachery from any group of them, throw back their covenant to them, so as to be on equal terms". [Al- Anfal: 57/58]

And said:

وَإِنْ جَنَحُوا لِلسَّلْمِ فَاجْنَحْ لَهَا
وَتَوَكَّلْ عَلَى اللَّهِ

"But if they incline to peace, you also incline to it and trust in Allah". [Al- Anfal: 61]

And He ﷻ said:

يَاأَيُّهَا الَّذِينَ آمَنُوا أَوْفُوا بِالْعُقُودِ

"Oh you who believe, fulfil your covenants". [Al- Maidah: 1]

And said:

$$وَلَا تَأْكُلُوا أَمْوَالَكُمْ بَيْنَكُمْ
بِالْبَاطِلِ وَتُدْلُوا بِهَا إِلَى الْحُكَّامِ
لِتَأْكُلُوا فَرِيقًا مِنْ أَمْوَالِ النَّاسِ
بِالْإِثْمِ وَأَنْتُمْ تَعْلَمُونَ$$

"And eat up not one another's property unjustly nor give bribery to the rulers that you may knowingly eat up a part of the property of others sinfully". [Al- Baqarah:188]

And He ﷻ said:

$$وَلَكُمْ فِي الْقِصَاصِ حَيَاةٌ يَاأُولِي الْأَلْبَابِ$$

"And indeed you have in Qisas life for you, Oh men of understanding". [Al- Baqarah: 179]

And,

$$وَالسَّارِقُ وَالسَّارِقَةُ فَاقْطَعُوا أَيْدِيَهُمَا جَزَاءً بِمَا كَسَبَا نَكَالًا مِنْ اللَّهِ$$

"As for the thief male or female, cut off his or her hand, a retribution for their deed and an exemplary punishment from Allah". [Al- Maidah: 38]

And,

$$فَإِنْ أَرْضَعْنَ لَكُمْ فَآتُوهُنَّ أُجُورَهُنَّ$$

"If they breastfeed for you, give them their wages". [At- Talaq: 6]

And,

$$\text{لِيُنفِقْ ذُو سَعَةٍ مِنْ سَعَتِهِ وَمَنْ قُدِرَ عَلَيْهِ رِزْقُهُ فَلْيُنفِقْ مِمَّا آتَاهُ اللَّهُ}$$

"Let each man spend according to his means and the man whose resources are restricted let him spend according to what Allah has given him". [At- Talaq: 7]

He ﷺ said:

$$\text{خُذْ مِنْ أَمْوَالِهِمْ صَدَقَةً تُطَهِّرُهُمْ}$$

"Take from their wealth charity to purify them". [At- Tauba: 103]

So, we find the guidelines for the civil, military, criminal, political and financial legislation clearly present in hundreds of ayat, in addition to the abundant authentic Ahadith. All were revealed to be ruled by, implemented and executed. As a matter of fact, they were put into practice at the time of the Messenger, ﷺ the *Khulafa'a ar-Rashideen* and those who came after them from the Muslim rulers. This clearly proves that Islam is a system of ruling and state, for society, life, the *Ummah* and individuals.

The above also shows that the state does not have the right to govern unless it functions in accordance with the Islamic system. Islam does not exist in a living fashion until it is embodied in a state that implements it's rules. Islam is a Deen and an ideology and ruling is a part of it. The state is the only legitimate method that Islam designated to carry out it's rules in public life. Islam cannot actually exist in a living fashion unless it has a state that implements it in all situations. It is a human political state, and not a spiritual divine one. It is not sacred nor is it's head infallible.

The ruling system of Islam comprises: the structure of the state, it's character, foundations, pillars, institution, the basis it is built on, the thoughts, concepts, and criterions the state uses to care for the affairs, and the constitution and canons that it implements.

It is a specific and distinctive system for a specific and distinctive state. It is completely different from all existing ruling systems in the world. This difference is seen in the basis the systems are established on, the thoughts, concepts and yardsticks that the affairs are cared for by, the forms that they are represented by, and the constitutions and canons which they implement.

18

The Ruling System in Islam is One of Unity and is Not Federal

I slam mandates unity amongst the Islamic countries and forbids them to form a federation or a confederation. The true and correct system of ruling is the system of unity, no other. This is due to the fact that Islam mandated it and forbade every other. The Messenger ﷺ said, "**And whoever gives a** *Baya'ah* **to an Imam, giving him the clasp of his hand and the fruit of his heart, he should obey him. If another disputes with him, then kill the other**". He ﷺ also said, "**If two Khulafaa are given the Baya'ah, then kill the latter of them**". The first hadith forbids dividing the state and directs us to forbid it's division even by the sword. The second hadith prohibit's making one state into many states, thus allowing no more than one Khalifah. Consequently, the ruling system in Islam is a system of unity, not federation. It is definitely haram to adopt other than the system of unity, and therefore, the federal union is definitely haram to adopt.

It is known that the federal union is an agreement between two or more states to unify some of their affairs that pertain to ruling while remaining as separate entities. Each of these states may withdraw from unifying all or some of these affairs whenever they desire. The federal union is not unity. It is characterised by the fact that each state may remain as an entity. The first step towards it's formation is electing a federal parliament and drafting a constitution for the federation, where the federation states define the affairs over which to unify. The constitution may determine the unification of judicial legislation, administrative laws, foreign policy, army, or economics...etc. It may decide the unification of state institutions while the entities continue to exist, as in the case of the United States. Also, it may direct that the states institutions remain independent but unify some affairs such as in the former Soviet Union. Thus, the constitution sets the type of federation which in turn must be approved by the federal parliament, as well as the parliament of each state, assuming they have one. So the federal state will have the authority designated by the constitution. The remaining authority continues to belong to the individual states, and therefore, each state continues to be a separate and distinct entity.

This is the reality of the federal union. Therefore, cancelling passports between two states, or developing economic unity, or unifying the education curriculum or legislation has no relationship with the federal union. These might take place between states that are not part of a federation. Similarly, it is not part of the federal union when a parliament or parliaments or conferences or sheikhdoms decide to establish such a union amongst themselves. Such a decision is merely an expression of desire. What matters is what the constitution determines regarding the type of union, it's state, and it's power.

Consequently, Islam does not permit the federal system at all, regardless of it's type, because the Islamic ruling system is a system of unity, and not union. Also, sovereignty in Islam belongs to the Shari'ah. The Shari'ah determines the ruling system, legislation and finance. No one has the authority to lay out any aspect of them. In addition, the rules of Shari'ah are the same for every Muslim. So, a different legislation is not allowed. Finance is the same for all Muslims. Expenses of Muslims come from the treasury house regardless of whether their lands have revenues or not. Jihad is an obligation upon Muslims, they are obliged to go for Jihad in case any Islamic land is attacked. So, Muslims have one entity whether they like it or not. Their legislation, finance, and anything related to ruling is one and cannot vary. The ruling system and system of life for Muslims is one of unity, not a union. Consequently, Islam mandates a system of a unified entity, not a system of various entities. It forbids union, obliges unity, and obliges war to achieve it.

19
The Public Responsibilities

The Law-Giver ﷺ determined the public responsibilities of the ruler with such clarity that left no room for ambiguity or misunderstanding. He ﷺ explained the ruler's responsibilities as a ruler, and his responsibilities with regards to his relationship with the citizens.

As for the ruler's responsibility to himself as a ruler, it is evident in the hadith in which the Messenger ﷺ explained some of the ruler's qualities. The most prominent of which are strength, *Taqwa*, kindness with the citizens and not to be repulsive. The Messenger ﷺ said that the ruler must be strong, not weak, and that the weak one is not fit to be a ruler. Muslim reported from Abu Tharr that the Messenger ﷺ said, "**Oh Abu Tharr, I see you a weak man and I desire for you what I desire for myself. Do not be the** *Ameer* **of two people, and do not administer the wealth of an orphan**". Also Abu Tharr narrated "I said: Oh Allah's Messenger, should you not use me"? He said, "He struck my shoulder with his hand and said, "**Oh Abu Tharr, you are weak and it is a trust, and on the Day of Judgement it is humiliation and sorrow, except to the one who took it** *(Imaarah)* **justly and fulfilled it's duties upon him**". Strength here refers to the strength of the personality, i.e. the mentality and the disposition.

Therefore, the ruler's mentality must be one of ruling, with which he comprehends matters and relations. His *Nafsiyyah* must be one of ruling, with which he realises that he is an *Ameer*, and so conducts his emotions accordingly. Since the strength of personality tends to dominate and control, he must possess a quality that would prevent him from the evil of domination. Therefore, he must have *Taqwa* regarding himself and regarding his caring for the *Ummah*. Sulayman ibn Buraydah reported from his father that he said, "The Messenger upon appointing an *Ameer* of an army or an expedition advised him to have *Taqwa* regarding himself and be good to the Muslims with him". Once the ruler has *Taqwa*, fear of Allah, and is watchful of Allah 🕮 in secret and publicly, this will deter him from treating the subjects despotically. *Taqwa,* however, does not stop him from being harsh and tough because being watchful of Allah 🕮 obliges him to abide by His commands. Since the nature of ruling is harshness and toughness, Allah 🕮 commanded the ruler to be lenient and cause no hardship to the subjects. Aishah (ra) said, "I heard Allah's Messenger say in my house, "**Oh Allah! Whoever is given a responsibility of leadership to my Ummah and inflicts hardship upon them, inflict hardship upon him. And whoever treats them kindly be kind with him**". The law-giver 🕮 also ordered the ruler to be someone who gives good news (*Mubashir*), and not someone that repels (scares away) the people (*Munaffir*). Abu Musa reported that He 🕮 said, "**Be *Mubashir* and not *Munaffir*. And treat with ease, with no hardship**".

This is with regard to the personal qualities of the ruler. As for his relationship with the subjects, the Law-giver commanded him to give them sincere advice and warned him against any mishandling of public funds. The Law-giver commanded him to rule his subjects with Islam mixed with nothing else. Allah 🕮 forbade paradise to the ruler who gives no advice to the people or who takes any of it's rights. Maqil ibn Yasar said, I heard the Prophet 🕮 say, "**Anyone whom Allah commissioned with the caretaking of people and does not give them his sincere advice, he will not smell the fragrance of paradise**". Maqil ibn Yasar also said, "I heard Allah's Messenger 🕮 say, "**Anyone who is in charge of the Muslims and does not try his utmost and give them his advice, will not enter paradise with them**". Also, Abu Said said, "Allah's Messenger 🕮 said, "**Every traitor will have a flag on the Day of Judgement that will be raised as high as his treachery. There is no treachery greater than that of the leader of the masses**". Therefore, trying one's utmost for the subjects and giving them advice is emphasised by the Messenger, 🕮 which shows how great the responsibility is.

As for mishandling public funds, Islam warned against it severely. When the Messenger 🕮 saw that one of his governors mishandled the funds, he reprimanded him and gave a public address in this regard. Abu Humayd Assaaidi reported that the Prophet appointed Ibn Al-Lutbiyah to collect the *Sadaqat* (alms) of Bani Salim. Upon his arrival, the Messenger 🅱 audited him, and the man said, "This is for you and this is a gift given to me". The Messenger 🅱 said, **"Why don't you sit in your parents house till you receive the gift, if you are truthful?"** Then the Messenger 🅱 addressed the people saying, after praising Allah, **"I appoint men from amongst you to discharge matters which Allah made me in charge of. One of you would come and say, this is for you and this is a gift that was given to me. Should he not sit in his parents house and wait to receive his gift, if he were truthful? By Allah, if any of you takes something without due right, he will come on the Day of Judgement carrying it (on his neck)"**. This means, Allah 🅰 will account him and punish him for his action. This is a strict warning against the mishandling of public funds by the ruler in any fashion, even by depending on misinterpretation or legal justification.

As for the rules (laws) that the ruler must rule by, the Law-giver 🅰 determined them. The ruler must rule by the Book of Allah 🅰 and the Sunnah of His Messenger 🅱. Allah 🅰 gave him the right to perform *Ijtihad* in the Qur'an and Sunnah, but forbade him from looking (to ruling) with other than Islam or to ever adopt from other than Islam. With regard to ruling by the Qur'an and the Sunnah exclusively, it is clear in the ayaat of the Qur'an. Allah 🅰 says,

$$\text{وَمَنْ لَمْ يَحْكُمْ بِمَا أَنزَلَ اللّٰهُ فَأُوْلَٰئِكَ هُمُ الْكَافِرُونَ}$$

"And those who rule not by that which Allah has revealed are Kafirs". [Al- Maidah: 44]

$$\text{وَمَنْ لَمْ يَحْكُمْ بِمَا أَنزَلَ اللّٰهُ فَأُوْلَٰئِكَ هُمُ الظَّالِمُونَ}$$

"And those who rule not by that which Allah has revealed are Fasiqs". [Al- Maidah: 45]

وَمَنْ لَمْ يَحْكُمْ بِمَا أَنزَلَ اللَّهُ
فَأُوْلَٰئِكَ هُمُ الْفَاسِقُونَ

"And those who rule not by that which Allah has revealed are Thalims".
[Al- Maidah: 47]

These ayaat are definite in restricting ruling to only that which Allah revealed. Allah ﷻ revealed to His Messenger ﷺ the Qur'an in words and meaning, and revealed the Sunnah in meaning not words.

Therefore, the ruler is restricted in his ruling to the Qur'an and the Sunnah. The Legislator permitted *Ijtihad* in the Book and Sunnah, i.e., exerting one's utmost effort in understanding and deducing laws from them. It was reported that when the Messenger ﷺ sent Muaath to Yemen, he asked him, **"What will you rule by"**? He said, "The Book of Allah". He ﷺ said, **"What if you did not find it"**? He said, "The Sunnah of Allah's Messenger". He ﷺ said **"What if you did not find it?"** He said "I will make *Ijtihad*. He ﷺ said, **"Alhumdulillah that he guided the Messenger of Allah's Messenger to that which is liked by Allah and His Messenger"**. In addition, the Law-giver rewarded the mistake of the ruler in *Ijtihad*. This encourages the ruler to engage in *Ijtihad* and refrain him from rigidity by limiting him to the apparent means of the text. Bukhari reported that Amr ibn Al-Aas said that he heard the Messenger of Allah ﷺ say, **"If the ruler rules and does *Ijtihad* and derives the right rule, he will be rewarded twice. And if he rules and performs *Ijtihad* and makes a mistake, he will be rewarded once"**. The Law-giver ﷺ specified that the rules by which the ruler rules with is Islam and none other. Despite the fact that it gave the ruler the right to perform *Ijtihad* even if he commit's a mistake, it stressed the fact that the rules must be from Islam only. Not only that, it forbade ruling by any other rules, it also forbade the seeking of rules from non-Islamic sources or to mix any other matter with Islam. Allah ﷻ said, addressing the Messenger ﷺ;

وَأَنْ احْكُمْ بَيْنَهُمْ بِمَا أَنزَلَ اللَّهُ
وَلَا تَتَّبِعْ أَهْوَاءَهُمْ وَاحْذَرْهُمْ أَنْ
يَفْتِنُوكَ عَنْ بَعْضِ مَا أَنزَلَ اللَّهُ
إِلَيْكَ

"So rule among them by that which Allah has revealed and follow not their desires instead of the truth that came to you". [Al- Maidah: 49]

And He ﷻ said

فَاحْكُمْ بَيْنَهُمْ بِمَا أَنزَلَ اللَّهُ وَلَا
تَتَّبِعْ أَهْوَاءَهُمْ عَمَّا جَاءَكَ مِنْ
الْحَقِّ

"And rule among them by that which Allah brought down, and follow not their desires, and be on guard that they might sway you from some of what Allah has revealed to you". [Al- Maidah: 48]

Since the speech directed to the Messenger ﷺ is directed to the *Ummah*, this speech is for every ruler. Also, Muslim reported that Aisha said, "Allah's Messenger ﷺ said, "**Whoever brings in our matter (*Deen*) that which is not part of it, it is rejected**". In another report from her, the Messenger ﷺ said "**Whoever does an action that is not of our matter (Deen), it is rejected**". In addition, Al-Bukhari reported from Ubaydullah, the son of Abdullah that Ibn Abbas said, "How could you ask the people of the Book about their legislation while your Book that was revealed to Allah's Messenger is more recent. You read it pure and unadulterated and it has informed you that the people of the Book changed and altered the Book of Allah ﷻ and wrote it with their own hands saying "It is from Allah" for a cheap price. Should not the knowledge you have received have prevented you from asking them?" The above texts make clear what the ruler is to rule by. The responsibility regarding the ruler is restricted to ruling by that which Allah ﷻ revealed.

These mandatory responsibilities of the ruler show that the Law-giver ﷺ defined the general responsibilities in a most clear fashion. These responsibilities upon the ruler are inclusive to every ruler, be he a Khalifah, his Assistant, Governor or District Governor (*Aamel*). Every one of them is a ruler and is restricted in his responsibilities. Since, these responsibilities are those of *Walis* and *Ameers* as well as other rulers, they are also the responsibilities of the Khalifah. This is because if they are mandatory on an *Ameer,* then they apply with greater reason to the general *Ameer,* the Khalifah.

The Messenger's ﷺ saying: "**There is no servant given the responsibility of subjects**", and "**Whoever is given any leadership responsibility of my Ummah**" and "**The worst of traitors is an Ameer of the public**", and Allah Taa'la's saying *"And whoever does not rule.."*. are all general. Their utterance includes the governor and the *Khalifah.* And the speech of the Messenger ﷺ is a speech to every ruler, *Khalifah* or governor. Also, the Messenger ﷺ explained the responsibility of the *Khalifah* towards his subjects in the hadith. Al-Bukhari reported that Abdullah ibn Umar said that Allah's Messenger ﷺ said, "**Each of you is in charge and each of you is responsible for his subjects: The imam of the people is in charge and he is responsible for his subjects; and the man is in charge of the people in his house and he is responsible for his subjects; the woman is in charge of her husbands household and children and she is responsible for her subjects; and the man's slave is in charge of his master's wealth and he is responsible for it. All of you are in charge and all of you are responsible for your subjects**". This hadith gave the *Khalifah* the general responsibility of all of his subjects. Therefore, general responsibilities are upon the ruler and thus upon the Khalifah.

The Law-giver ﷺ fully guaranteed the discharge of the general responsibilities by the rulers by directing him and by legislation. As for directing him, he is warned of Allah's punishment if he did not carry out or was even negligent in his responsibilities. It showed that it amounts to humiliation and sorrow on the Day of Judgement if *Imaarah* is assumed by a weak person who does not give it it's due right. The Messenger prayed to Allah ﷺ to make things hard upon anyone who makes things hard on the Islamic *Ummah.* Allah ﷺ forbade paradise to anyone who did not give the *Ummah* his sincere advice. These are but a few of the warnings that were given to the ruler showing his final abode, namely Allah's punishment, if he did not fulfil his responsibilities. The Shari'ah did not stop at that point, it went further by appointing the *Ummah* as guardian over the ruler, to see that he carries out his responsibilities. It commanded her to bear arms against him if he rules by anything other than Islam, and if *Kufr* becomes clear. It stated that whoever is killed in the process of objecting to the *Munkar* of the ruler, he is the leader of martyrs. Allah's Messenger ﷺ said, "**The leader of martyrs is Hamzah and a man who stood up to an unjust ruler, commanded him (to do good) and forbade him (from doing evil) and he (the ruler) killed him**". Islam made anyone who accepts the shortcomings of the ruler and follows him, responsible in front of Allah ﷻ and unsafe from His ﷻ punishment. Muslim reported that Ummu Salamah said that Allah's Messenger ﷺ said, "**There will be leaders from whom you will recognise (some of their actions) and reject (some.) Whoever recognises then he is clear and whoever rejects he is safe, but those who accept and follow...**". The second report explains the first one. An-Nawawi explained this hadith by saying, "It means, and Allah ﷻ knows best, that whoever recognises the evil (munkar) with no ambiguity, he will have a way to become clear of it's sin and punishment, namely by changing it with his hand or mouth. If unable, then let him hate it in his heart. His saying, **"Whoever rejects is safe"**, means that whoever is unable to change it with his hand or mouth and thus rejects it in his heart and hates it he will be safe against sharing the sin with them. **"but those who accept and follow"**, means that whoever accepts their action in his heart and follows them in their action, he is not clear nor safe.

In this hadith, the Messenger ﷺ commanded us to denounce the evil actions of the ruler. He obliged this to be carried out by any possible means of the hand on the condition that it does not reach fighting, i.e. without using arms. It is to be carried out with the mouth with any speech, or with the heart if unable to use the hand or the mouth. The Law-giver considered anyone who does not denounce the rulers bad action as his partner in sin, for he said that whoever accepts what they do and follows them in their action, he will not be clear or safe from the sin. However, such rejection and denouncement, applies when they do something haram while they rule by Islam in general. In the case where they no longer implement Islam and execute the rules of *Kufr*, it is not sufficient to denounce them by the hand and the mouth and the heart. Islam made fighting with arms the way to change their action. In the hadith of Ummu Salameh which was reported by Muslim, it says, "They said: should we not fight them? He said, **"No, as long as they pray"**. In another report, "Should we not fight them, Oh Messenger of Allah? He said, **"No, as long as they establish Salat (prayer) amongst you"**. In another report, " We said: Oh Messenger of Allah, should we not fight them when they do that (rule by haram)? He said, **"No, as long as they establish Salah (prayer) amongst you"**. Al-Bukhari reported that Ubaadah ibn As-Samit said, "The Prophet ﷺ called us and we gave him the Bayah. He said, "Part of what he took our pledge to do was to hear and obey, whether we were active or lazy, we were in ease or hardship... and not to go against the people in authority. He ﷺ said, **"Unless you see clear *Kufr*, you have a clear evidence from Allah ﷻ regarding it"**. The understanding of these Ahadith is that we fight the people in charge if we see clear *Kufr*, and we fight them with the sword if they do not establish salah (prayer). Establishing salah (prayer) regarding the ruler is indicative for ruling by Islam. In other words, as long as they rule by Islam there is no fighting or bearing arms or rebellion. If they rule by other than Islam, then they must be fought against. By these measures, Islam has completely guaranteed the discharge of the general responsibilities.

20

Detachment between the Ummah and the State,
and the Obligation of Accounting

It is noticeable today that the *Ummah* is completely detached from the state, i.e. the rulers. Also, the relationship between the masses and the rulers is one between two separate and different parties, not one between subjects and the state. Moreover, in addition to the relationship being between two different and separate parties, it is a relationship characterised by hatred, conflict and contradiction, in which there exists no approachment either now or for the foreseeable future. This weakens the *Ummah* and the state, because people without a guardian will have a weak structure; and a state without the backing of it's people will be weak, requiring little effort to remove it, will be dependent upon the help of the *Ummah*'s enemies.

This detachment between the *Ummah* and the state was natural and obligatory when the disbelieving states used to rule the lands directly, i.e. in the days of British colonialism. Now that British authority is officially over, and those who rule the lands are Muslims from the Islamic *Ummah*, there is no reason for this detachment to continue. The relationship between the masses and the state should have changed into one between the guardian and subjects and to full attachment between the people and the guardian. In reality, however, this detachment has remained and continues to remain. The rulers continue to be a class that is different from the *Ummah*. Both parties have remained against each other. The *Ummah* views the rulers as her enemies as she viewed the British, and it is possible she feels that their injustice is more than that of the British. The rulers view the *Ummah* as collaborators against them, who want to destroy them and who are their enemy. They plot against her and she plots against them. This places the *Ummah* in a state of hopelessness which prevents her from moving even one step forward towards glory and tranquility. This also confines the rulers' thinking to whatever maintains their ruling seats, even if they have to use the help of the foreigner. It makes them think not of elevating the *Ummah* except hypocritically, and by using methods that keep her declined, and always in a state of weakness, so that they stay in control over her.

This situation of detachment between the *Ummah* and the state results from the *Ummah*'s negligence of her obligation to account the rulers, as well as her lack of awareness that she is the origin of authority. Had the *Ummah* been aware that she was the origin of authority, and had she fulfilled her obligation decreed upon her by Allah ﷻ of accounting the rulers, then a ruler who is an enemy of hers and a traitor would never lead her affairs. Nor would there exist between her and the rulers such detachment, or would she be in such a state of weakness, fragmentation, and backwardness. She would not have remained under the actual influence of the disbelievers, even if apparently ruled directly by a Muslim from amongst her. Therefore, for the *Ummah* to become one entity with the state, and one class with the ruler, she must account the rulers, say the *Haqq* (truth) and work hard and resolve to change the situation of the rulers or change them altogether. If the *Ummah* does not engage in that, she will undoubtedly continue to decline with increasing speed (as is now seen) until she almost perishes.

Islam made it obligatory upon the Muslims to account the rulers. It commanded them to account the rulers and say the truth wherever they are, with no fear of blame for the sake of Allah ﷻ. In the second *Bay'ah* of Aqabah, the Muslims pledged to the Messenger ﷺ to say the *Haqq* with no fear. The text of the *Bay'ah* states, "And we should say the *Haqq* wherever we are with no fear of any blame for the sake of Allah". As for accounting the rulers, commanding them to do good and forbidding them from doing evil, in addition to that being included in the ayaat of commanding good and forbidding evil, there are explicit texts commanding Muslims to account them. Attiyyah reported about Aby Said who said that Allah's Messenger ﷺ said: **"The best jihad is a word of haqq (truth) to an unjust ruler".** Abu Umamah said "A man approached Allah's Messenger ﷺ at the first *Jamrah* (stone-at Mina) and asked: Oh messenger of Allah, which jihad is best? The Messenger ﷺ kept silent. When the Messenger ﷺ threw the second *Jamrah* (stone) the man asked him again, but the Messenger ﷺ kept silent. After the

Messenger ❀ threw the *Jamrah* (stone) of Aqabah, and he was about to ride, he ❀ said: **"Where is the questioner"**. The man said , " It is me, 'O Messenger of Allah. The Messenger said: **"A word of Haqq said to an unjust ruler"**. This is a direct text that obliges Muslims to address the ruler, to tell him the *Haqq* and to account him. Moreover, the Messenger ❀ encouraged us to struggle against the unjust rulers, regardless of the harm that may result, even if it leads to death. It was reported that Allah's Messenger ❀ said: **"The master of the martyrs is Hamzah ibn Abdil Muttalib and a man who stood up to an unjust ruler, commanded him (to do the good and refrain from evil) and so he (the ruler) killed him"**. This is the most profound form of expression: urging the endurance of harm to the point of death, in accounting the rulers and struggling against the tyrant rulers.

Struggling against the current oppression of the rulers and accounting them for all their actions, their treachery and conspiracies against the *Ummah* is an obligation from Allah ❀ upon all Muslims. Carrying out this obligation is what eliminates the barrier between the *Ummah* and the rulers. It is what makes the *Ummah* and the rulers one bloc, and it guarantees changing the situation of the rulers, as well as changing them if required. This is the first step in the way for revival. *Nahdah* (revival) cannot be achieved unless ruling is established based on the Islamic Aqeedah. And there is no way to achieve this except by confronting and accounting the unjust rulers.

21

Establishing Political Parties is a Fard Kifayah

Accounting the rulers as Allah ﷻ commanded Muslims to do may be carried out by individuals, groups or blocs. As Allah ﷻ commanded Muslims to call to Islam, command good and forbid evil and accounting the ruler, He ﷻ also commanded them to establish political blocs from among them. These blocs (as groups) would call to *Al-khayr*, i.e. Islam, command good and forbid evil and account the rulers. Allah ﷻ said,

وَلْتَكُنْ مِنْكُمْ أُمَّةٌ يَدْعُونَ إِلَى
الْخَيْرِ وَيَأْمُرُونَ بِالْمَعْرُوفِ
وَيَنْهَوْنَ عَنِ الْمُنْكَرِ

"And let there be from among you be a group that calls to Al-Khayr and commands good and forbids evil". [Al- Imran: 104]

Meaning, Oh you Muslims, establish a group from amongst you, that has the characteristics of a group, and performs two functions: the function of calling to Islam, and the function of commanding good and forbidding evil.

The command to form a group is a decisive command, for the task of the *Jam'ah* that the ayah detailed is an obligation upon Muslims, as established by the various ayaat and Ahadith. The obligatory task of the group serves as a *Qareenah* (proof), which makes the command of establishing the group decisive. Consequently, the command in the ayah is one of obligation. It is *Fard Kifayah* (of sufficiency) upon the Muslims, meaning, if this obligation is carried out by the few, the rest would be exempt from it. It is not a personal fard on each Muslim. This is due to the fact that Allah ﷻ commanded the Muslims to establish from amongst them a group whose task is to call to *Al-khayr* and command good and forbid evil. He did not command the Muslims as a whole to do these functions. He merely commanded them to establish a group from amongst them to fulfil this obligation. So the subject of the command in the ayah is focused upon the establishment of the group, not upon the two functions. Both of the functions are only an explanation of the actions of the group, Allah ﷻ commanded to be established, and thus they are a description of the type of group that is required to be established.

For the group to be a group that is able to engage in it's task as a group, it must have certain qualities so as to be and remain to be a group while performing it's task. In order for it to be a group, there must exist a bond that links it's members together to form one body, i.e. a bloc. Without such a bond, the required group to be established cannot exist and function as a group. Also, for the group to remain as such while working, it must have an Ameer who must be obeyed. This is because the Shar'a commanded every group who has more than two members to have an Ameer. Allah's Messenger ﷺ said, **"It is not permitted for three people in open country (travelling) not to have one of them as Ameer"**.

These two characteristics, namely the bond among the group and the presence of an Ameer who must be obeyed, indicate that the saying of Allah ﷻ, *"And let there be from amongst you a group"* means let there be from amongst you a group that has a bond among it's members, and an Ameer who must be obeyed. This is the group, or bloc, or party, or association, or any name that is given to the group, that has to satisfy what is required to be a group and to continue to be a group while working. It is evident therefore, that the ayah is a command to establish parties, blocs, associations or organisations, etc.

With respect to the command in the ayah to establish a group this means to establish political groups; this understanding is taken from the fact that the ayah defined the group's task, as to call for Islam and command good and forbid evil. The task of commanding good and forbidding evil is mentioned in general terms and thus it includes commanding the rulers to do good and forbidding them from doing evil. This means it is an obligation to account them. Accounting the rulers is a political action performed by political parties. As a matter of fact, it is one of the most important functions of political parties. Therefore, the ayah indicates that it is obligatory to form political parties to call to Islam, command good and forbid evil, and to account the rulers for their actions and activities.

The ayah also indicates that these parties must be Islamic parties founded on the Islamic Aqeedah and adopting the *Ahkaam shariah* (divine rules). It is not allowed for these parties to be communist, socialist, capitalist, nationalistic, or patriotic and they are not allowed to call for democracy, secularism, or free masonry. Nor is it allowed to be founded on anything but the Islamic Aqeedah or to adopt other than divine rules. This is because the ayah has defined the characteristics of these parties by specifying the actions they perform. These actions are the call to Islam and the commanding of good and the forbidding of evil. For any party to indulge in such actions, it must carry Islam, be based on Islam, and adopt the rules of Islam. It is impossible for any group which is founded on a communist, socialist, capitalist, democratic, secular, masonic, nationalistic, patriotic or a regional basis to be based on Islam, or carry Islam or adopt the *Ahkam* of Islam. Any of this would be based on *Kufr* and structured upon the thoughts of *Kufr*.

Therefore, it is prohibited for Muslims to structure themselves on the basis of communism, socialism, capitalism, democracy, secularism, masonry, nationalism, patriotism, or upon any basis other than the basis of Islam.

Furthermore, for these parties to achieve the aim required of them, they must be public and not secret. This is because calling for *Al-khayr*, commanding good, and the forbidding of evil, accounting the rulers and working to hold the reigns of power through the *Ummah*, are all explicit and open actions, and must not be carried out in secret or in hiding. In addition, the actions of these parties must not be physical, because their functions are verbal. They invite to Islam verbally, and command good and forbid evil verbally. Therefore, their means must be peaceful. They should not bear arms or resort to violence as a means in their actions. Raising arms against the ruler is not allowed due to the ahaadeeth that forbade that. So, commanding good and forbidding evil, and accounting the ruler is to be done peacefully and without raising arms against them.

The only situation when arms are to be raised against the ruler is when he makes clear *Kufr* of which we have proof from Allah ﷻ. This is reported in the hadith of Ubaadah ibn Assamit, "And not to contest against those in command". He ﷺ said, "**unless you see clear and obvious *Kufr* of which you have a clear proof from Allah**".

22
How can Individuals & Parties Influence
International Politics & the State's direction?

A question might be raised: how can individuals influence world politics and how can parties influence the state's direction, especially as such direction is deep-rooted and has existed for centuries? The answer: when individuals or parties pursue the political actions and understand international politics, they should not do so for rational pleasure, intellectual luxury or for the purpose of education and increasing knowledge. Rather they should follow it in order to care for the world's affairs and in order to decide how to influence the world. In other words, they do it in order to be politicians. Far be it from the politician that he seeks the rational pleasure, even if he is of the greatest intellect, and far be it from him to incline to the intellectual luxury even if he is of the deepest thinkers. So, the politician follows up (pursues) politics and understands the international situation and the internal position and pursues the international politics solely because he is a politician, not because he is an intellectual or a thinker. Being a politician means that he strives to care for the world's affairs, i.e. to influence international politics. This is on the one hand, on the other hand, a politician does not work while viewing himself as an individual, he functions as part of an *Ummah*, and as part of an entity, i.e. in a state. Even though he is not one of those who decides upon or executes the states policies, he is eager to be one of them and accounts those who do so. Consequently, he will have an international influence even if he remains an individual with no decision-making or executive responsibilities. If he acted as such he will have an influence, because the state, which he belongs to, influences the world through people like him. He amy also together with people like him, strive to make state influence international politics.

This will lead to what is called the fruit's of political concepts, namely making the state influence international politics and the international situation by developing politically aware individuals who comprehend the political actions that take place in the world, especially by the superpowers. Consequently, the first step towards influencing international politics and the international situation is to crystallise the political concepts. The first obstacle is to motivate individuals to pursue political actions and understand international politics, i.e. to create politicians of international politics. As a result the state will naturally influence the international political situation. This manifests the level of importance that political concepts have and how valuable they are.

It must be known, however, that the state will not be present internationally, unless and until it maintains relations with the other states. The individual in a society will not be present in his society unless and until he maintains relations with the other individuals. His status in society and among the people is according to these relations and according to his influence on these relations amongst the people. Similarly, the state's presence is established through it's relations with the other states. It's status is affected positively or negatively in accordance with it's relations with states and it's influence on international relations.

23
Democracy is a System of Kufr

Democracy is a ruling system that was laid down by people to resolve the ruling problem they had at the time. At that time, people used to suffer the oppression of rulers who claimed they were God's representatives on earth. The rulers claimed that they ruled the people with God's authority, thus it was God who gave the ruler authority over the people. In other words, the ruler received his authority from God. In reaction, philosophers and thinkers started discussing the subject of ruling and laid down a system to rule the people. This system was the democratic system. So the democratic system was laid down to rid the people from the oppression of the rulers. This system dictates that the ruler receives his authority from the people, not from God and that the people are the ones who appoint him to rule them with their consent. Democracy is one of the ideas laid down by the West for the cultural invasion of Muslim countries. In the Berlin Conference, held in the late 18th century to divide the Ottoman state (the "sick man of Europe"), the West could not agree on it's division. However, they agreed to force it to adopt the democratic system. Only then did the Khilafah introduce the system of the Sadr a'atham (prime minister) and ministers, which is part of the democratic system.

Upon the abolition of the Khilafah in the early twentieth century, the West enhanced it's efforts in the Muslim countries to attack the Islamic ideas with the democratic system. As a result books were written describing Islam as the Deen of democracy, and democracy became introduced as part of Islam. Also, when the West changed it's style of colonialism to the new one where it erected states and rulers, it made the democratic system the basis for them. As a result, many states have been established on the basis of the democratic system. While it is true that in the beginning of the twentieth century, they used to invite to democracy on the premise that it is part of Islam, (since Islam still had importance and was valued in the hearts of the Muslims) today, however, they no longer claim that democracy is part of Islam. Rather they give it to the people as a ruling system, so the people take it only as a ruling system, and nothing more. Even those who claim that they want Islam, want to adopt democracy and call for it.

Democracy is the rule of the people, by the people, for the people. This means that, the people in a society unite among themselves in order to create the public will. This is done when each individual holds an agreement to belong to the community he lives amongst. This is called the Social Contract. According to this contract, each individual is to completely recede all his rights to the whole community. Each individual of the people is to contribute with his person and all his ability to the chief administration of the public will. From this contract, there will result a collective conventional body which is the political body or the state, whether it is called a republic or otherwise. Democracy therefore, means that all the people are the state. Each individual has equal rights to the others with regards to establishing the state, appointing rulers and making laws as well as anything else that is related to ruling and the state. So by the contract which each person has with himself, he has completely receded all his rights and liberties to the community to which he belongs. This community or collective contract is the public will, and the sovereignty. Thus, according to this the people are everything.

The origin of the democratic system is that the people are considered to comprise public will and sovereignty. It is the people who have the authority to legislate and choose the rulers. The people alone have the authority in everything in the state and in the country. So the source of public will and sovereignty as well as everything else, is the people. The people are the masters of themselves, and rule themselves by themselves. The people means all the individuals in a country regardless of their affiliation, religion, or language, as long as they are humans.

Thus, sovereignty, is the public will, which is the state. Therefore, the state is the people as a whole and the people are the masters of themselves. They are sovereign and they are the public will. However, this public will is something that is conventional. In order for the people to discharge their interests, they choose a government to be the executive power. Consequently, in the state there will be two bodies: legislative, which lays down the laws, and executive which is chosen by the community to execute it's will, i.e. it's laws.

Since the people as a whole cannot be the legislative body, they choose representatives to serve as the legislative body. These representatives make up parliament. Therefore, the parliament in the democratic system is the body that represents the public will. It chooses the government and the head of state acts as ruler and a representative of the community to execute the public will. Therefore, the democratic system means that the people are masters of themselves. They lay down the laws and they choose the government. Consequently, prior to manipulation, democracy was composed of two authorities: the public will or the people, and the government chosen by the people to execute their will. After manipulation, democracy has three authorities: the legislative authority represented by the parliament, the executive authority represented by the government, and the judicial authority represented by the judges or the supreme court.

These three authorities constitute the state. The legislative authority is the people's representatives, the judicial authority is the body which judges by the laws, and the executive authority is the body that implements the rulings of the judges and the laws decided by the parliament. The three authorities are independent and do not interfere in the affairs of each other. Democracy however in it's true meaning, never existed nor will it ever exist. For the people to always gather to look into all public affairs is impossible, to actually rule is impossible, and to engage in executing their will is impossible. That is why they disguised the idea of democracy, manipulated it, and invented what is called the government, the head of state and the parliament. They said that democracy is the rule of the people, by the people, for the people. Such a statement is inaccurate. The people are not in charge of anything. The one who is in charge of all affairs is the head of state or the government.

Democracy is forbidden to be adopted for three reasons. Firstly, those behind it's idea and propagation are the West. This is a form of cultural invasion, in fact it is a cultural invasion. Therefore, whoever accepts it is actually submitting to the cultural invasion and hence contributes to it's success. In order to struggle against the cultural invasion as a whole, and specifically against democracy, democracy must be fought and rejected. Also, those who are pushing for democracy in terms of it's implementation are the colonialist West. When the West wanted to change the form of colonialism, it established states on the basis of democracy. So, whoever endorses it is actually propagating and supporting colonialism, the Western system, and the rulers whom the colonialists appointed in their place. Therefore, struggling to completely terminate colonialism, obliges fighting against the system that secures it's presence, which is the democratic system.

Secondly, democracy is a fanciful idea that cannot be implemented. When they twisted it in order to implement it, deception became the basis for their misinterpretation. The parliament does not legislate, rather the government propose the laws and the parliament passes them. The parliament does not choose the government. It is chosen by the head of the state. The parliament merely approves the formation which is a mere formality. Moreover, the ruler in any democratic country is not the parliament which represents the people, but the head of state or government. Eventually, ruling can only be in the hand of one person, so how can the people rule? Therefore, democracy contradicts the reality of ruling and it is in conflict with life. Consequently, democracy is a fanciful idea, impossible to implement, is based on lies and misinterpretation and leads the people astray.

Thirdly, democracy is man-made. It is laid down by humans for humans. Since a human is liable to error, and it is Allah ﷻ alone who does not make mistakes, then only the system that is from Allah ﷻ should be taken. Hence, adopting democracy and rejecting the system of Allah ﷻ is an error that leads to disaster.

Also, the democratic system is a *Kufr* system because it is not *Ahkaam Shariyah* (divine rules). The ruling system in Islam is *Ahkaam Shariyah* from Allah ﷻ. Therefore, the democratic system is a system of *Kufr*. Accordingly, ruling by the democratic system is calling for a system of *Kufr*. It is not allowed under any circumstances to call for or adopt the democratic system.

Moreover, the democratic system conflicts with and contradicts the ruling system of Islam. Islam has nothing to do with democracy. While the *Ummah* is the one who appoints the ruler, it has no authority to depose him. The Law-giver is Allah ﷻ not humans, the people or the

Ummah. Authority over the people and the rulers as well as sovereignty belongs only to the Law-giver 鐵. Since the democratic system gave sovereignty to people, the right to choose the ruler and to legislate, then it contradicts with the ruling system of Islam. Islam gave the *Ummah* the right to choose the ruler but with no right to depose him. In addition, Islam gave the sovereignty to the shariyah, not to the people, and made the law-maker only Allah.鐵 Consequently, the democratic system contradicts the ruling system of Islam and therefore, it is haram to adopt it or call for it.

24

The Political Issue for the Ummah and the Islamic State

The term "political issue" means the issue which faces the state and the *Ummah* and needs to be addressed as part of looking after their affairs. This issue might be general and therefore, it will be the main political case, or it may be specific whereby it will be simply political case. It might also be part of an issue and then it will be a single question out of several questions related to the case. For example, the issue that faces the Islamic *Ummah* and obliges her to carry out caretaking actions, is the re-establishment of Khilafah in life. This matter is therefore, the political case. Other issues that exist, such as the issues of Palestine and the Caucasus are questions included in this case. This is true, even though these are issues that face the *Ummah* and demand a solution and caretaking. However, they are part of the establishment of the Khilafah. Once the Islamic state is established, it's political case will be implementing Islam internally and carrying it's call to the world. When it implements Islam perfectly, and it's character becomes strong internationally, then it's political case will be to carry the Islamic Da'wah to the whole world until Allah ﷻ makes Islam prevail over all other deens.

Therefore, the political case is the important and fundamental issue that shar'a obliges the state and the *Ummah* to address and execute. Therefore the state must act to do what the shariyah requires of it to do in it's regard. This needs no specific evidence since it is part of the concept of applying the rules of shariyah on occurring events. Consequently, the political case varies in accordance with the occurring events.

The political case for the Prophet ﷺ in Makkah while calling for Islam was to make it prevail. That is why Abu Talib said to the Messenger ﷺ, "Your people came to me and said so and so, so save me and yourselves, and burden me not with that which I can not afford". The Messenger thought that his uncle was letting him down. The Messenger ﷺ said, **"Oh uncle, by Allah, if they were to put the sun in my right hand and the moon in my left hand, so that I leave this matter, I will not leave it until Allah makes it prevail or I die for it"**. Such a statement reflects that the political case for the Messenger at that time was to make Islam prevail.

When the Prophet ﷺ moved to Madinah and established the state he engaged in several battles against his main enemy, the head of *Kufr* Quraysh, so the political case for him continued to be to make Islam prevail. Due to this, on his way to Hajj and before he arrived at Hudaybiyah, he heard that Quraysh had heard of his journey and come out to fight him. A man from Bani Ka'ab said to him, "They heard of your trip and they prepared themselves for you and put on their tiger skins (became furious). They camped in Thee Tuah, pledged to Allah that they will never let you enter". The Messenger ﷺ replied, **"Woe to Quraysh, they are destroyed by war. What do they have to lose if they left the matter between me and the other Arabs"**. And continued to say **"What does Quraysh think? By Allah will continue to do jihad for what He sent me with until Allah makes it prevail or my neck will be detached"**. The detachment of his neck refers to death, i.e. until he dies. The political case in both situations is one. In Makkah, he insisted on calling to Islam until Allah ﷺ made it prevail, while in Madinah, i.e. after the establishment of the state, he insisted to continue jihad until Allah made it prevail.

Once the Messenger ﷺ struck the peace treaty with Quraysh, (which was a great conquest since it facilitated the conquest of Makkah, and the Arabs started entering into the Deen of Allah ﷺ in large numbers) and the political case for the Messenger ﷺ became not only to make Islam prevail, but to make it victorious over all deens, that is to prevail over e.g. the Romans and the Persians.

In this regard, Allah ﷻ revealed the Surah of Al-Fath which had the ayat;

$$هُوَ الَّذِي أَرْسَلَ رَسُولَهُ بِالْهُدَى وَدِينِ الْحَقِّ لِيُظْهِرَهُ عَلَى الدِّينِ كُلِّهِ$$

"It is He who sent His Messenger with guidance and the Deen of Haqq to make it prevail over all deens". [Al- Fath: 28]

Based on the above, once the Islamic state implements Islam perfectly and it's character becomes strong internationally, it's political case becomes to make Islam prevail over all other deens and to prepare to destroy all other ideologies and deens.

25
The Vital Issue

The situation of the Muslims today is felt by every Muslim. It needs no explanation or elaboration. These countries are ruled by systems of *Kufr*. They are definitely *Dar-ul-Kufr*. They are divided into more than fifty entities, in the form of states, emirates, sultanates or sheikhdoms. They are all too weak to stand in the face of the Kuffar. That is why the case in each Muslim country is to change it to Dar-ul-Islam and unify it with the other Islamic countries. This is the vital issue. As a matter of fact, it is at the heart of all the vital issues. So this issue should be dealt with as a matter of life and death. This vital issue, i.e. the changing of every Islamic land to *Dar-ul-Islam* and unifying it with the other Islamic lands, is a goal that we must strive to achieve. The method used to achieve this goal is the establishment of the Khilafah as a ruling system through which the country is changed to Dar-ul-Islam and then unified with the other Islamic lands.

It must be clear however, that the challenge which Muslims face now is not merely to appoint a Khalifah, so as to say that this is fard *Kifayah* upon Muslims, due to what is reported by Ibn Umar that the Prophet said: **"and whosoever dies without having an Imam of the Muslim community (Jama'ah) over him, he will die the death of Jahiliyyah".** Some would then say that this is not a vital issue. This is an invalid argument because the challenge that faces the Muslims today is the establishment of the Khilafah. In other words, Muslims now must establish the Khilafah system as a ruling system. This is different from appointing a Khalifah, even though establishing the system of Khilafah includes the appointment of a Khalifah. Establishing the Khilafah is definitely the vital issue, for, in addition to it being the method to change our lands from lands of *Kufr* to one of Islam, it's establishment removes *Kufr* systems i.e. the clear and open *Kufr*. This is a vital issue due to the saying of Allah's Messenger 鑅, **"Unless you see clear *Kufr*,"** "it was said: Should we not fight them?" He 鑅 said: **"No, as long as they**

establish salat amongst you". Therefore, the method to achieve the vital issue is also itself a vital issue, because it is the method of achieving a vital issue. Also, legal evidence from the Sunnah shows that it is a vital issue. Therefore, the measures taken toward it must be viewed as a matter of life or death. Since the Muslims were ruled by *Kufr*, and their affairs were run by the *Kuffar*, hypocrites and apostates, they have been trying to liberate themselves from *Kufr*, it's masters and helpers. But they have missed the point that what they are struggling for is a vital issue that has one measure only, that of life and death. Due to this lack of comprehension, the Muslims, in their capacity as a community or *Ummah*, have not been prepared to endure harm, imprisonment and torture, let alone poverty, destruction and death in it's pursuit. All of these cannot be detached from the struggle for the vital issues. As a result, these attempts have been doomed to fail and the *Ummah* has not been able to move one step forward towards the case she has been struggling for.

Muslims, since the first moment, did not need much thinking and contemplation to conclude that their issue is a vital issue. This is still clear now. It is impossible intellectually and eventually for the *Kuffar* to allow Islam to return to political life - the ruling position - as long as they have the least power to strike full upon those who are working for it. The apostates and the hyprocrites are no less criminals than the *Kuffar*. They will do whatever is within their ability to engage in war against the believers who want to strip them of the ruling to establish the rules of Allah 畿 and protect Allah's sanctities.

Consequently, it is impossible for any attempt by Muslims regarding this issue to bear fruit's, unless they consider this issue a vital one, which can't be achieved without certain measures. Due to the fact the that Muslims did not comprehend the nature of the battle, or the rule of Allah 畿 regarding it, they attempted to liberate themselves in a manner that is not at the level of a vital issue, but as an ordinary case. Hence, the measures they took were less than that of life and death. The truth of the matter is that the issue which is vital by nature, such as abolishing the system of *Kufr* and establishing the system of Islam, whether comprehended as such or not, is impossible to achieve by anyone regardless of his strength and effort unless he considers it in his actions and concepts and adopted towards it the measures naturally required by it, namely the measures of life and death. Therefore, Muslims, as individuals and groups, must struggle, and they must regard their actions in the struggle against *Kufr* as a matter of life and death, because the nature of their issue requires this, and because the shar'a represented in the Book and the Sunnah decided this level of actions.

However, Allah's Messenger 🕮 taught us how to define our issues and to take the measure of life and death in every vital issue. When Allah 🕮 sent him 🕮 with Islam and he 🕮 started to convey the message via an intellectual struggle, he 🕮 defined the issue as making Islam prevail, and he took towards it the measures of life and death. It was reported that when the Messenger's uncle Abu Talib told Muhammad 🕮 what Quraysh had asked of him (to make Muhammad 🕮 stop his *Da'wah*), and said to him:
"Your people came to me and said so and so, so save me and yourselves, and burden me not with that which I cannot afford" the Messenger 🕮 said: "**Oh uncle, by Allah, if they put the sun in my right hand and the moon in my left hand so that I leave this matter, I will not leave it until Allah makes it prevail or I die for it**". When he established the state, and performed Jihad, he defined his issue to also be the triumph of Islam. He took towards it the measure of life and death. It was reported that when the Messenger 🕮 was in *Asafan,* not far away from Makkah, on his way to *Umrah,* during the incident of *Hudaybiyah,* a man from Bani Ka'ab met him. The Messenger 🕮 asked him if he had any news of Quraysh. The man answered, "Quraysh heard of your journey so they went out to meet you wearing the skin of tigers (becoming furious). They are camping in Thee-tuwa pledging to Allah that you will never enter Makkah. Their horsemen are led by Khalid ibn Al Walid are at Kira'a Al-Ghameem. The Messenger 🕮 said: "**Woe to Quraysh! They are destroyed by war. What do they have to lose if they let the matter between me and the other Arabs? If they (the Arabs) kill me, then that is what they wanted, and if Allah makes me prevail over them, they will enter into Islam unhurt. And if they do not, they will fight while strong. What does Quraysh think? By Allah, I will continue my Jihad for that which Allah sent me with until Allah makes it prevail or this neck is detached**". This is taken to mean death. He 🕮 then continued on his trip until he reached Hudaybiyah.

In both cases i.e. the case of carrying the Da'wah with the intellectual struggle, and the case of carrying the Da'wah by the sword and Jihad, the

Messenger ﷺ defined the issue as making Islam prevail and he made it a vital issue. In both cases he took the measure required by namely that of life and death. Due to this, he ﷺ said in the first case, "**Until Allah makes it prevail or I die for it**", and in the second case, he ﷺ said: "**Until Allah makes it prevail or my neck be detached**". Had the Messenger ﷺ not taken the measure of life and death towards it, Islam would not have considered that case as a vital issue and not succeeded, either in conveying the Da'wah by the intellectual struggle nor by Jihad and the sword. Similarly today, where the systems of *Kufr* are controlling the Muslims, the Kuffar and the hypocrites dominate them, if Muslims do not consider this issue a vital one and do not take the measure of life and death regarding it, it is not possible for their struggle to bear fruit's, or for them to move even one step forward.

Therefore, we call upon every Muslim in the midst of this *Kufr* that is dominating the lands of Islam to work to establish the Khilafah as the method to change his land to Dar-ul-Islam, unify it with the other Islamic lands and carry the Da'wah to the world so that Islam prevails. We call upon every Muslim to repeat with true Iman and enlightened awareness the saying of the Messenger, ﷺ "**By Allah, if they put the sun in my right hand and the moon in my left hand so as to leave this matter, I will not leave it until Allah makes it prevail or I die for it**". And his saying , "**By Allah I will continue doing my Jihad for the matter which Allah has sent me with until Allah makes it prevail or this neck becomes detached**".